Prayer

St. Alphonsus M. Liguori, CSSR

P R A Y E R

The Great Means of Salvation and Perfection

Edited by Rev. Eugene Grimm, CSSR

SOPHIA INSTITUTE PRESS

Manchester, New Hampshire

Sophia Institute Press
Box 5284, Manchester, NH 03108
1-800-888-9344

www.SophiaInstitute.com

Sophia Institute Press® is a registered trademark of Sophia Institute.

paperback ISBN 978-1-64413-542-6

ebook ISBN 978-1-64413-543-3

Library of Congress Control Number: 2021938704

First printing

To the Incarnate Word,
Jesus Christ,
the Beloved of the Eternal Father,
the Blessed of the Lord,
the Author of Life,
the King of Glory,
the Savior of the World,
the Expected of Nations,
the Desire of the Eternal Hills,
the Bread of Heaven,
the Mediator between God and Man,
the Master of Virtues,
the Lamb without Spot,
the Man of Sorrows,
the Eternal Priest,
the Victim of Love,
the Home of Sinners,
the Fountain of Graces,
the Good Shepherd,
the Lover of Souls,

Alphonsus the sinner
consecrates this book.

Dedication to Jesus and Mary

O Incarnate Word, Thou hast given Thy Blood and Thy Life to con-fer on our prayers that power by which, according to Thy promise, they obtain for us all that we ask. And we, O God, are so careless of our salvation that we will not even ask Thee for the graces that we must have if we should be saved! In prayer Thou hast given us the key of all Thy divine treasures; and we, rather than pray, choose to remain in our misery. Alas! O Lord, enlighten us and make us know the value of prayers, offered in Thy name and by Thy merits, in the eyes of Thy Eternal Father. I consecrate to Thee this my book; bless it, and grant that all those into whose hands it falls may have the will to pray always and may exert themselves to stir up others also to avail themselves of this great means of salvation.

To thee also do I recommend my little work, O Mary, great Mother of God: patronize it, and obtain for all who read it the spirit of prayer, and of continual recourse in all their necessities to thy Son, and to thee, who art the Dispenser of graces, the Mother of mercy, and who never leavest unsatisfied him who recommends himself to thee, O mighty Virgin, but obtainest from God for thy servants whatever thou askest.

Contents

Part III
Mental Prayer

Editor's Note

This book, which was published in 1759, is one of the most important works of St. Alphonsus.... He speaks thus: "This book, though small, has cost me a great deal of labor. I regard it as of extreme utility to all sorts of persons and I unhesitantly assert that among all spiritual treatises, there is none and there can be none more necessary than that which treats on prayer as a means of obtaining eternal salvation."

—Rev. Eugene Grimm, CSSR

Foreword

No one questions the preeminent status of St. Teresa of Ávila and St. John of the Cross as masters of prayer and the interior life. These two great saints are Doctors of the Church because their teaching is vital for the life of the whole Church, regardless of what spiritual tradition the student finds himself in.

This, of course, captures what a Doctor of the Church is. All Doctors are saints, but they are saints whom the Church holds up as having something to say that is unique and powerful and who should shape the way the Church thinks about the matters they address in their writings. In fact, most of the doctrine of the Church comes from or is centrally influenced by the Doctors of the Church.

There is an informal subset of these Doctors who are often referred to as "Spiritual Doctors" of the Church. This is because their particular realm of insight brings light to the spiritual life—the interior life of faith of all believers. In terms of what it means to be an authentic disciple of Jesus—particularly in the realm of prayer—St. Alphonsus Liguori stands shoulder to shoulder with the two giants mentioned above.

In the recent past, the works of St. Alphonsus have faded into the background. With the resurgence of interest in preconciliar teaching on matters of liturgy and the interior life, however, this great saint's works are beginning to resurface. This is very good news for the spiritual and theological health of the Church in our time.

I have no doubt that, in this book, even if you are well informed in matters of the interior life, you will be surprised and challenged by the clarity and bold claims St. Alphonsus makes regarding prayer: its necessity, its power, and how it enables us to progress in working out our salvation.

No serious student of the interior life can afford to pass up the profound wisdom of this great Doctor of the interior life. May you discover or rediscover what it means to be a man or woman of prayer as you sit at the feet of this spiritual and theological giant. May you be drawn ever more deeply into the heart of God as you allow St. Alphonsus Liguori to lead you there.

—Dan Burke
President of the Avila Institute for Spiritual Formation

Prayer

Part I

The Necessity, Power, and Conditions of Prayer

Chapter 1

The Necessity of Prayer

1. Prayer Is a Means Necessary to Salvation

One of the errors of Pelagianism was the assertion that prayer is not necessary for salvation. Pelagius, the impious author of that heresy, said that man will only be damned for neglecting to know the truths necessary to be learned. How astonishing! St. Augustine said: "Pelagius discussed everything except how to pray,"[1] though, as the saint held and taught, prayer is the only means of acquiring the science of the saints; according to the text of St. James: "If any man lacks wisdom, let him ask of God, who gives to all abundantly, and upbraids not" (James 1:5). The Scriptures are clear enough in pointing out how necessary it is to pray if we would be saved. "We ought always to pray and not to faint" (Luke 18:1). "Watch and pray, that you enter not into temptation" (Matt. 26:41). "Ask, and it shall be given you" (Matt. 7:7). The words "we ought," "pray," "ask," according to the general consent of theologians, impose the precept and denote the necessity of prayer. Wickliffe said that these texts are to be understood, not precisely of prayer, but only of the necessity of

[1] *De Nat. et Grat.* c. 17.

Prayer

good works, for in his system, prayer was only well doing; but this was his error and was expressly condemned by the Church. Hence Lessius wrote that it is heresy to deny that prayer is necessary for salvation in adults, as "it evidently appears from Scripture that prayer is the means without which we cannot obtain the help necessary for salvation."

The reason of this is evident. Without the assistance of God's grace, we can do no good thing: "Without me, you can do nothing" (John 15:5). St. Augustine remarks on this passage, that Our Lord did not say, "Without me, you can complete nothing,"[2] but "without me, you can do nothing"; giving us to understand that without grace we cannot even begin to do a good thing. Nay more, St. Paul writes that of ourselves we cannot even have the wish to do good. Not that we are sufficient to think anything ourselves, but our sufficiency is from God (2 Cor. 3:5). If we cannot even think a good thing, much less can we wish it. The same thing is taught in many other passages of Scripture: "God works all in all" (1 Cor. 12:6). "I will cause you to walk in my commandments, and to keep my judgments, and do them" (Ezek. 36:27). So that, as St. Leo I says, "Man does no good thing, except that which God, by his grace, enables him to do,"[3] and hence the Council of Trent says: "If anyone shall assert that without the previous inspiration of the Holy Spirit, and His assistance, man can believe, hope, love or repent, as he ought, in order to obtain the grace of justification, let him be anathema."[4]

The author of the *Opus Imperfectum* says that God has given to some animals swiftness, to others claws, to others wings, for

[2] *Contra ep. pel.* 1. 2. C. 8.
[3] *Cone. Araus.* ii. cap. 20.
[4] Session 6, Can. 3.

the preservation of their life; but He has so formed man that God Himself is his only strength. So that man is completely unable to provide for his own safety, since God has willed that whatever he has, or can have, should come entirely from the assistance of His grace.

But this grace is not given in God's ordinary providence except to those who pray for it; according to the celebrated saying of Gennadius: "We believe that no one approaches to be saved, except at the invitation of God; that no one who is invited works out his salvation, except by the help of God; that no one merits this help, unless he prays."[5] From these two premises, on the one hand, that we can do nothing without the assistance of grace; and on the other, that this assistance is only given ordinarily by God to the man that prays, who does not see that the consequence follows that prayer is absolutely necessary to us for salvation? And although the first graces that come to us without any cooperation on our part, such as the call to faith or to penance, are, as St. Augustine says, granted by God even to those who do not pray; yet the saint considers it certain that the other graces, and specially the grace of perseverance, are not granted except in answer to prayer: "God gives us some things, as the beginning of faith, even when we do not pray. Other things, such as perseverance, He has only provided for those who pray."[6]

Hence it is that the generality of theologians, following St. Basil, St. Chrysostom, St. Clement of Alexandria, St. Augustine, and other Fathers, teach that prayer is necessary to adults, not only because of the obligation of the precept (as they say), but because it is necessary as a means of salvation. That is to say, in

[5] *De Eccl. Dogm.* c. 26.
[6] *De dono pers.* c. 16.

Prayer

the ordinary course of Providence, it is impossible that a Christian should be saved without recommending himself to God and asking for the graces necessary to salvation. St. Thomas teaches the same: "After Baptism, continual prayer is necessary to man, in order that he may enter Heaven; for though by Baptism our sins are remitted, there still remain concupiscence to assail us from within, and the world and the devil to assail us from without" (III, q. 39, art. 5). The reason, then, which makes us certain of the necessity of prayer is shortly this: in order to be saved, we must contend and conquer: "He that strives for the mystery is not crowned except he strive lawfully" (2 Tim. 2:5). But without the divine assistance we cannot resist the might of so many and so powerful enemies: now this assistance is only granted to prayer; therefore without prayer there is no salvation.

Moreover, that prayer is the only ordinary means of receiving the divine gifts is more distinctly proved by St. Thomas in another place, where he says that whatever graces God has from all eternity determined to give us, He will give only if we pray for them. St. Gregory says the same thing: "Man by prayer merits to receive that which God had from all eternity determined to give him."[7] Not, says St. Thomas, that prayer is necessary in order that God may know our necessities, but in order that we may know the necessity of having recourse to God to obtain the help necessary for our salvation and may thus acknowledge Him to be the author of all our good. As, therefore, it is God's law that we should provide ourselves with bread by sowing corn and with wine by planting vines, so has He ordained that we should receive the graces necessary to salvation by means of prayer: "Ask, and it shall be given you; seek, and you shall find" (Matt. 7:7).

[7] *Dial. l.* I, c. 8.

We, in a word, are merely beggars who have nothing but what God bestows on us as alms: "But I am a beggar and poor" (Ps. 39:18). The Lord, says St. Augustine, desires and wills to pour forth His graces upon us but will not give them except to him who prays: "God wishes to give, but only gives to him who asks." This is declared in the words, Seek, and it shall be given to you. Whence it follows, says St. Teresa, that he who seeks not does not receive. As moisture is necessary for the life of plants, to prevent them from drying up, so, says St. Chrysostom, is prayer necessary for our salvation. Or, as he says in another place, prayer vivifies the soul, as the soul vivifies the body: "As the body without the soul cannot live, so the soul without prayer is dead and emits an offensive odor." He uses these words because the man who omits to recommend himself to God at once begins to be defiled with sins. Prayer is also called the food of the soul because the body cannot be supported without food; nor can the soul, says St. Augustine, be kept alive without prayer: "As the flesh is nourished by food, so is man supported by prayers."[8] All these comparisons used by the holy Fathers are intended by them to teach the absolute necessity of prayer for the salvation of everyone.

2. Without Prayer It Is Impossible to Resist Temptations and to Keep the Commandments

Moreover, prayer is the most necessary weapon of defense against our enemies; he who does not avail himself of it, says St. Thomas, is lost. He does not doubt that Adam fell because he did not recommend himself to God when he was tempted: "He sinned because he had not recourse to the divine assistance" (I, q. 94,

---

[8] *De sal. Doc.* c. 28.

Prayer

art. 4). St. Gelasius says the same of the rebel angels: "Receiving the grace of God in vain, they could not persevere, because they did not pray."[9] St. Charles Borromeo, in a pastoral letter, observes that among all the means of salvation recommended by Jesus Christ in the Gospel, the first place is given to prayer; and he has determined that this should distinguish his Church from all false religions, when he calls her "the house of prayer."[10] "My house is a house of prayer" (Matt. 21:13). St. Charles concludes that prayer is "the beginning and progress and the completion of all virtues." So that in darkness, distress, and danger, we have no other hope than to raise our eyes to God and, with fervent prayers, to beseech His mercy to save us: "As we know not," said king Josaphat, "what to do, we can only turn our eyes to you" (2 Chron. 20:12). This also was David's practice, who could find no other means of safety from his enemies than continual prayer to God to deliver him from their snares: "My eyes are ever towards the Lord; for he shall pluck my feet out of the snare" (Ps. 24:15). So he did nothing but pray: "Look upon me, and have mercy on me; for I am alone and poor" (Ps. 25:16). "I cried to You, O Lord; save me that I may keep Your commandments" (Ps. 118:146). Lord, turn Your eyes to me, have pity on me, and save me; for I can do nothing, and beside You there is none that can help me.

And, indeed, how could we ever resist our enemies and observe God's precepts, especially since Adam's sin, which has rendered us so weak and infirm, unless we had prayer as a means whereby we can obtain from God sufficient light and strength to enable us to observe them? It was a blasphemy of Luther's to say that after the sin of Adam the observance of God's law has

---

[9] *Tr. adv. pelag. haer.*
[10] *Litt. past. de or. in comm.*

become absolutely impossible to man. Jansenius also said that there are some precepts which are impossible even to the just, with the power which they actually have, and so far his proposition bears a good sense; but it was justly condemned by the Church for the addition he made to it, when he said that they have not the grace to make the precepts possible. It is true, says St. Augustine, that man, in consequence of his weakness, is unable to fulfill some of God's commands with his present strength and the ordinary grace given to all men; but he can easily, by prayer, obtain such further aid as he requires for his salvation: "God commands not impossibilities, but by commanding He suggests to you to do what you can, to ask for what is beyond your strength; and He helps you, that you may be able." This is a celebrated text, which was afterward adopted and made a doctrine of faith by the Council of Trent. The holy Doctor immediately adds, "Let us see whence?" (i.e., how man is enabled to do that which he cannot). "By medicine he can do that which his natural weakness renders impossible to him."[11] That is, by prayer we may obtain a remedy for our weakness; for when we pray, God gives us strength to do that which we cannot do of ourselves.

We cannot believe, continues St. Augustine, that God would have imposed on us the observance of a law and then made the law impossible. When, therefore, God shows us that of ourselves we are unable to observe all His commands it is simply to admonish us to do the easier things by means of the ordinary grace which he bestows on us, and then to do the more difficult things by means of the greater help which we can obtain by prayer. "By the very fact that it is absurd to suppose that God could have commanded us to do impossible things, we are admonished what to

[11] *De Natura et gr.* c. 43.

do in easy matters, and what to ask for in difficulties."[12] But why, it will be asked, has God commanded us to do things impossible to our natural strength? Precisely for this, says St. Augustine, that we may be incited to pray for help to do that which of ourselves we cannot do. "He commands some things which we cannot do, that we may know what we ought to ask of him."[13] And in another place: "The law was given, that grace might be sought for; grace was given that the law might be fulfilled."[14] The law cannot be kept without grace, and God has given the law with this object, that we may always ask Him for grace to observe it. In another place he says: "The law is good, if it be used lawfully; what, then, is the lawful use of the law?" He answers: "When by the law we perceive our own weakness, and ask of God the grace to heal us."[15] St. Augustine then says: We ought to use the law; but for what purpose? To learn by means of the law, which we find to be above our strength, our own inability to observe it, in order that we may then obtain by prayer the divine aid to cure our weakness.

St. Bernard's teaching is the same: "What are we, or what is our strength, that we should be able to resist so many temptations? This certainly it was that God intended: that we, seeing our deficiencies, and that we have no other help, should with all humility have recourse to His mercy."[16] God knows how useful it is to us to be obliged to pray, in order to keep us humble, and to exercise our confidence; and He therefore permits us to

---

[12] *De Natura et gr.* c. 69.
[13] *De Gr. et Lib. Arb.* c. 16.
[14] *De Spir. et Litt.* c. 19.
[15] Sermon 156, Ed. Ben.
[16] *In Quad.* s. 5.

be assaulted by enemies too mighty to be overcome by our own strength, that by prayer we may obtain from His mercy aid to resist them; and it is especially to be remarked that no one can resist the impure temptations of the flesh without recommending himself to God when he is tempted. This foe is so terrible that, when he fights with us, he, as it were, takes away all light; he makes us forget all our meditations, all our good resolutions; he makes us also disregard the truths of faith and even almost lose the fear of the divine punishments. For he conspires. with our natural inclinations, which drive us with the greatest violence to the indulgence of sensual pleasures. He who in such a moment does not have recourse to God is lost. The only defense against this temptation is prayer, as St. Gregory of Nyssa says: "Prayer is the bulwark of chastity"[17] and before him Solomon: "And as I knew that I could not otherwise be continent except God gave it, I went to the Lord and besought him" (Wisd. 8:21). Chastity is a virtue which we have no strength to practice unless God gives us; and God does not give this strength except to him who asks for it. But whoever prays for it will certainly obtain it.

Hence St. Thomas observes (in contradiction to Jansenius) that we ought not to say that the precept of chastity, or any other, is impossible to us; for though we cannot observe it by our own strength, we can by God's assistance. "We must say that what we can do with the divine assistance is not altogether impossible to us" (I-II, q. 109, art. 4). Nor let it be said that it appears an injustice to order a cripple to walk straight. No, says St. Augustine, it is not an injustice, provided always means are given him to find the remedy for his lameness; for after this, if he continues to go crooked, the fault is his own: "It is most wisely

---

[17] *De Or. Dom.* i.

commanded that man should walk uprightly, so that when he sees that he cannot do so of himself, he may seek a remedy to heal the lameness of sin."[18] Finally, the same holy Doctor says that he will never know how to live well who does not know how to pray well. "He knows how to live aright who knows how to pray aright";[19] and, on the other hand, St. Francis of Assisi says that without prayer you can never hope to find good fruit in a soul.

Wrongly, therefore, do those sinners excuse themselves who say that they have no strength to resist temptation. But "if you have not this strength, why do you not ask for it?" is the reproof which St. James gives them: You have it not, because you ask it not. There is no doubt that we are too weak to resist the attacks of our enemies. But, on the other hand, it is certain that God is faithful, as the apostle says, and will not permit us to be tempted beyond our strength: "God is faithful, who will not suffer you to be tempted above that which you are able; but will make also with the temptation issue, that you may be able to bear it" (1 Cor. 10:13). "He will provide an issue for it," says Primasius, "by the protection of His grace, that you may be able to withstand the temptation." We are weak, but God is strong; when we ask Him for aid, He communicates His strength to us, and we shall be able to do all things, as the apostle reasonably assured himself: "I can do all things in him who strengthens me" (Phil. 4:13). He, therefore, who falls has no excuse (says St. Chrysostom), because he has neglected to pray; for if he had prayed, he would not have been overcome by his enemies: "Nor can anyone be excused who, by ceasing to pray, has shown that he did not wish to overcome his enemy."[20]

---

[18] *De Perf. Just. hom.* c. 3.
[19] Sermon 55, E. B. app.
[20] Sermon de Moyse.

3. Invocation of the Saints

Is It Useful to Have Recourse to the Saints?

Here a question arises: whether it is necessary to have recourse also to the intercession of the saints to obtain the grace of God.

That it is a lawful and useful thing to invoke the saints, as intercessors, to obtain for us, by the merits of Jesus Christ, that which we, by our demerits, are not worthy to receive is a doctrine of the Church, declared by the Council of Trent: "It is good and useful to invoke them by supplication, and to fly to their aid and assistance to obtain benefits from God through His Son, Jesus Christ."[21]

Such invocation was condemned by the impious Calvin, but most illogically. For if it is lawful and profitable to invoke living saints to aid us, and to beseech them to assist us in prayers, as the prophet Baruch did: "And pray ye for us to the Lord our God "(Bar. 1:13) and St. Paul: "Brethren, pray for us" (1 Thess. 5:25); and as God Himself commanded the friends of Job to recommend themselves to his prayers, that by the merits of Job He might look favorably on them: "Go to my servant Job ... and my servant Job shall pray for you; his face I will accept" (Job 42:8); if, then, it is lawful to recommend ourselves to the living, how can it be unlawful to invoke the saints who in Heaven enjoy God face-to-face? This is not derogatory to the honor due to God, but it is doubling it, for it is honoring the King not only in His person but in His servants. Therefore, says St. Thomas, it is good to have recourse to many saints, "because by the prayers of many we can sometimes obtain that which we cannot by the prayers of one." And if anyone objects, "But why have recourse

---

[21] Sess. 25, *De inv. Sanct.*

to the saints to pray for us when they are already praying for all who are worthy of it?" the same Doctor answers that no one can be said to be worthy that the saints should pray for him, but that "he becomes worthy by having recourse to the saints with devotion."[22]

Is It Good to Invoke the Souls in Purgatory?

Again, it is disputed whether there is any use in recommending oneself to the souls in Purgatory. Some say that the souls in that state cannot pray for us; and these rely on the authority of St. Thomas, who says that those souls, while they are being purified by pain, are inferior to us, and therefore "are not in a state to pray for us, but rather require our prayers" (II-II, q. 83, art. 11). But many other Doctors, as Bellarmine, Sylvius, Cardinal Gotti, Lessius, Medina, and others, affirm with great probability that we should piously believe that God manifests our prayer to those holy souls in order that they may pray for us and so that the charitable interchange of mutual prayer may be kept up between them and us. Nor do St. Thomas's words present much difficulty; for, as Sylvius and Gotti say, it is one thing not to be in a state to pray, another not to be able to pray. It is true that those souls are not in a state to pray, because, as St. Thomas says, while suffering they are inferior to us and rather require our prayers; nevertheless, in this state they are well able to pray, as they are friends of God. If a father keeps a son whom he tenderly loves in confinement for some fault; if the son then is not in a state to pray for himself, is that any reason why he cannot pray for others? And may he not expect to obtain what he asks, knowing, as he does, his father's affection for him? So

[22] In 4, *Sent. dist.* 45, q. 3, a. 2.

the souls in Purgatory, being beloved by God, and confirmed in grace, have absolutely no impediment to prevent them from praying for us. Still, the Church does not invoke them or implore their intercession, because ordinarily they have no cognizance of our prayers. But we may piously believe that God makes our prayers known to them; and then they, full of charity as they are, most assuredly do not omit to pray for us. St. Catherine of Bologna, whenever she desired any favor, had recourse to the souls in Purgatory and was immediately heard. She even testified that by the intercession of the souls in Purgatory she had obtained many graces which she had not been able to obtain by the intercession of the saints.

Our Duty to Pray for the Souls in Purgatory

Here let me make a digression in favor of those holy souls. If we desire the aid of their prayers, it is but fair that we should mind to aid them with our prayers and good works. I said it is fair, but I should have said it is a Christian duty; for charity obliges us to succor our neighbor when he requires our aid, and we can help him without grievous inconvenience. Now it is certain that amongst our neighbors are to be reckoned the souls in Purgatory, who, although no longer living in this world, yet have not left the communion of saints. "The souls of the pious dead," says St. Augustine, "are not separated from the Church,"[23] and St. Thomas says more to our purpose, that the charity which is due to the dead who died in the grace of God is only an extension of the same charity which we owe to our neighbor while living: "Charity, which is the bond which unites the members of the Church, extends not only to the living, but also to the dead who

---

[23] *De Civitate Dei* 1. 20, c. 9.

die in charity."[24] Therefore, we ought to succor, according to our ability, those holy souls as our neighbors; and as their necessities are greater than those of our other neighbors, our duty to succor them seems also to be greater.

But now, what are the necessities of those holy prisoners? It is certain that their pains are immense. The fire that tortures them, says St. Augustine, is more excruciating than any pain that man can endure in this life: "That fire will be more painful than anything that man can suffer in this life."[25] St. Thomas thinks the same and supposes it to be identical with the fire of Hell: "The damned are tormented and the elect purified in the same fire."[26] And this only relates to the pains of sense. But the pain of loss (that is, the privation of the sight of God), which those holy souls suffer, is much greater; because not only their natural affection, but also the supernatural love of God wherewith they burn, draws them with such violence to be united with their Sovereign Good that when they see the barrier which their sins have put in the way, they feel a pain so acute that if they were capable of death, they could not live a moment. So that, as St. Chrysostom says, this pain of the deprivation of God tortures them incomparably more than the pain of sense: "The flames of a thousand Hells together could not inflict such torments as the pain of loss by itself." So that those holy souls would rather suffer every other possible torture than be deprived for a single instant of the union with God for which they long. So St. Thomas says that the pain of Purgatory exceeds anything that can be endured in this life: "The pain of Purgatory must exceed all pain of this life." And

[24] In 4. *Sent. d.* 45. q. 2. s. 2.
[25] *In Ps.* 37.
[26] In 4. *Sent. d.* 21. I. a. I.

Dionysius the Carthusian relates that a dead person who had been raised to life by the intercession of St. Jerome told St. Cyril of Jerusalem that all the torments of this earth are refreshing and delightful when compared with the very least pain of Purgatory: "If all the torments of the world were compared with the least that can be had in Purgatory, they would appear comfortable."[27] And he adds that if a man had once tried those torments, he would rather suffer all the earthly sorrows that man can endure till the Day of Judgment than suffer for one day the least pain of Purgatory. Hence St. Cyril wrote to St. Augustine: "That as far as regards the infliction of suffering, these pains are the same as those of Hell—their only difference being that they are not eternal."[28] Hence, we see that the pains of these holy souls are excessive, while, on the other hand, they cannot help themselves; because as Job says: "They are in chains and are bound with the cords of poverty" (Job 36:8). They are destined to reign with Christ; but they are withheld from taking possession of their kingdom till the time of their purgation is accomplished. And they cannot help themselves (at least not sufficiently, even according to those theologians who assert that they can by their prayers gain some relief) to throw off their chains until they have entirely satisfied the justice of God. This is precisely what a Cistercian monk said to the sacristan of his monastery: "Help me, I beseech you, with your prayers; for of myself I can obtain nothing." And this is consistent with the saying of St. Bonaventure: "Destitution prevents solvency."[29] That is, those souls are so poor that they have no means of making satisfaction.

[27] *De Quat. Nov.* a. 53.
[28] *Int. Op. Aug. Ep.* 19. E. B. app.
[29] *Sermon de mort.*

Prayer

On the other hand, since it is certain, and even of faith, that by our suffrages, and chiefly by our prayers, as particularly recommended and practiced by the Church, we can relieve those holy souls, I do not know how to excuse that man from sin who neglects to give them some assistance, at least by his prayers. If a sense of duty will not persuade us to succor them, let us think of the pleasure it will give Jesus Christ to see us endeavoring to deliver His beloved spouses from prison, in order that He may have them with Him in Paradise. Let us think of the store of merit which we can lay up by practicing this great act of charity; let us think, too, that those souls are not ungrateful and will never forget the great benefit we do them in relieving them of their pains and in obtaining for them, by our prayers, anticipation of their entrance into glory; so that when they are there, they will never neglect to pray for us. And if God promises mercy to him who practices mercy toward his neighbor — "Blessed are the merciful, for they shall obtain mercy" (Matt. 5:7) — he may reasonably expect to be saved who remembers to assist those souls so afflicted and yet so dear to God. Jonathan, after having saved the Hebrews from ruin by a victory over their enemies, was condemned to death by his father, Saul, for having tasted some honey against his express commands; but the people came before the king and said, "Shall Jonathan then die, who hath wrought this great salvation in Israel?" (1 Sam. 14:45). So may we expect that if any of us ever obtains, by his prayers, the liberation of a soul from Purgatory, that soul will say to God: "Lord, suffer not him who has delivered me from my torments to be lost." And if Saul spared Jonathan's life at the request of his people, God will not refuse the salvation of a Christian to the prayers of a soul which is His own spouse. Moreover, St. Augustine says that God will cause those who in this life have most succored those holy souls, when they come to Purgatory themselves, to be most succored by others. I may here observe that, in practice, one of the best suffrages is to hear Mass for them and, during the holy Sacrifice, to recommend them to God by the merits and Passion of Jesus Christ. The following form may be used: "Eternal Father, I offer you this Sacrifice of the Body and Blood of Jesus Christ, with all the pains which He suffered in His life and death; and by His Passion I recommend to You the souls in Purgatory, and especially that of ..." the souls of all those who are at the point of death.

Is It Necessary to Invoke the Saints?

Whatever doubt there may be whether or not the souls in Purgatory can pray for us, and therefore whether or not it is of any use to recommend ourselves to their prayers, there can be no doubt whatever with regard to the saints. For it is certain that it is most useful to have recourse to the intercession of the saints canonized by the Church, who are already enjoying the vision of God. To suppose that the Church can err in canonizing is a sin or is heresy, according to St. Bonaventure, Bellarmine, and others; or at least next door to heresy, according to Suarez, Azorius, Gotti, etc.; because the Sovereign Pontiff, according to St. Thomas, is guided by the infallible influence of the Holy Spirit in a special way when canonizing the saints.

But to return to the question just proposed: Are we obliged to have recourse to the intercession of the saints? I do not wish to meddle with the decision of this question; but I cannot omit the exposition of a doctrine of St. Thomas. In several places above quoted, and especially in his book of Sentences, he expressly lays it down as certain that everyone is bound to pray because (as he asserts) in no other way can the graces necessary for salvation be obtained from God, except by prayer. "Every man is bound to pray, from the fact that he is bound to procure spiritual good for himself, which can only be got from God; so it can only be obtained by asking it of God."[30] Then, in another place of the same book, he proposes the exact question "Whether we are bound to pray to the saints to intercede for us?"[31] And he answers as follows—in order to catch his real meaning, we will quote the entire passage:

> According to Dionysius, the order which God has instituted for His creatures requires that things which are remote may be brought to God by means of things which are nearer to Him. Hence, as the saints in Heaven are nearest of all to Him, the order of His law requires that we who "remaining in the body are absent from the Lord," should be brought to Him by means of the saints; and this is effected by the divine goodness pouring forth His gifts through them. And as the path of our return to God should correspond to the path of the good things which proceed from Him to us, it follows that, as the benefits of God come down to us by means of the suffrages of the saints, we ought to be brought to God by the same way, so that a second time we may receive His benefits by the mediation of the saints. Hence it is that we make them our intercessors with God, and as it were our mediators, when we ask them to pray for us.

Note well the words "the order of God's law requires"; and especially note the last words: "as the benefits of God come down to ... us by means of the suffrages of the saints, in the same way we

---

[30] In 4, *Sent. d.* 15. q. 4. a. i.
[31] Dist. 45, q. 3, a. 2.

must be brought back to God so that a second time we may receive His benefits by the mediation of the saints." So that, according to St. Thomas, the order of the divine law requires that we mortals should be saved by means of the saints, in that we receive by their intercession the help necessary for our salvation. He then puts the objection that it appears superfluous to have recourse to the saints, since God is infinitely more merciful than they and more ready to hear us. This he answers by saying: "God has so ordered, not on account of any want of mercy on His part, but to keep the right order which He has universally established, of working by means of second causes. It is not for want of His mercy, but to preserve the aforesaid order in the creation."

In conformity with this doctrine of St. Thomas, the Continuator of Tourneley and Sylvius write that although God only is to be prayed to as the Author of grace, yet we are bound to have recourse also to the intercession of the saints, so as to observe the order which God has established with regard to our salvation, which is that the inferior should be saved by imploring the aid of the superior. "By the law of nature we are bound to observe the order which God has appointed; but God has appointed that the inferior should obtain salvation by imploring the assistance of his superior.'[32]

The Intercession of the Blessed Virgin

And if this is true of the saints, much more is it true of the intercession of the Mother of God, whose prayers are certainly of more value in His sight than those of all the rest of the inhabitants of Heaven together. For St. Thomas says that the saints, in proportion to the merits by which they have obtained grace for

[32] *De Relig.* p. 2, c. 2, a. 5.

themselves, are able also to save others; but that Jesus Christ, and so also His Mother, have merited so much grace that they can save all men. "It is a great thing in any saint that he should have grace enough for the salvation of many besides himself; but if he had enough for the salvation of all men, this would be the greatest of all; and this is the case with Christ, and with the Blessed Virgin."[33] And St. Bernard speaks thus to Mary: "Through you we have access to your Son, O discoverer of grace and Mother of salvation, that through you He may receive us, who through you was given to us."[34] These words signify that as we only have access to the Father by means of the Son, who is the Mediator of justice, so we only have access to the Son by means of the Mother, who is mediator of grace and who obtains for us, by her intercession, the gifts which Jesus Christ has merited for us. And therefore St. Bernard says, in another place that Mary has received a twofold fullness of grace. The first was the Incarnation of the Word, who was made Man in her most holy womb; the second is that fullness of grace which we receive from God by means of her prayers. Hence the saint adds: "God has placed the fullness of all good in Mary, that if we have any hope, any grace, any salvation, we may know that it overflows from her who 'ascends abounding with delights.'"[35] She is a garden of delights, whose odors spread abroad and abound; that is, the gifts of graces. So that whatever good we have from God, we receive all by the intercession of Mary. And why so? Because, says St. Bernard, it is God's will: "Such is His will, who would have us receive everything through Mary." But the more precise reason is deduced

---

[33] *Expos. in Sal. Aug.*
[34] *In Adv. Dom. s. 2.*
[35] *De Aquoed.*

from the expression of St. Augustine that Mary is justly called our Mother because she cooperated by her charity in the birth of the faithful to the life of grace, by which we become members of Jesus Christ, our Head: "But clearly she is the Mother of His members (which we are); because she cooperated by her charity in the birth of the faithful in the Church, and they are members of that Head."[36] Therefore, as Mary cooperated by her charity in the spiritual birth of the faithful, so also God willed that she should cooperate by her intercession to make them enjoy the life of grace in this world and the life of glory in the next; and therefore the Church makes us call her and salute her, without any circumlocution, by the names "our life, our sweetness, and our hope."

Hence St. Bernard exhorts us to have continual recourse to the Mother of God because her prayers are certain to be heard by her Son: "Go to Mary, I say, without hesitation; the Son will hear the Mother." And then he says: "My children, she is the ladder of sinners, she is my chief confidence, she is the whole ground of my hope."[37] He calls her the ladder because, as you cannot mount the third step except you first put your foot on the second, nor can you arrive at the second except by the first, so you cannot come to God except by means of Jesus Christ, nor can you come to Christ except by means of His Mother. Then he calls her his greatest security and the whole ground of his hope because, as he affirms, God wills that all the graces which He gives us should pass through the hands of Mary. And he concludes by saying that we ought to ask all the graces which we desire through Mary because she obtains whatever she seeks,

[36] *De S. Virginit.* c. 6.
[37] *De Aquoed.*

Prayer

and her prayers cannot be resisted. "Let us seek grace, and let us seek it through Mary, because what she seeks she finds and she cannot be disappointed."

The following saints teach the same as St. Bernard: St. Ephrem: "We have no other confidence than from you, O purest Virgin!"[38] St. Ildephonsus: "All the good things that the divine Majesty has determined to give them, He has determined to commit to your hands; for to you are entrusted the treasures and the wardrobes of grace."[39] St. Germanus: "If you desert us, what will become of us, O life of Christians?"[40] St. Peter Damian: "In your hands are all the treasures of the mercies of God."[41] St. Antoninus: "Who seeks without her aid, attempts to fly without wings."[42] St. Bernardine of Siena: "You are the dispenser of all graces; our salvation is in your hands." In another place, he not only says that all graces are transmitted to us by means of Mary but also asserts that the Blessed Virgin, from the time she became the Mother of God, acquired a certain jurisdiction over all the graces that are given to us: "Through the Virgin the vital graces are transfused from Christ, the Head, into His Mystical Body. From the time when the Virgin Mother conceived in her womb the Word of God, she obtained a certain jurisdiction (if I may so speak) over every temporal procession of the Holy Spirit; so that no creature could obtain any grace from God except by the dispensation of His sweet Mother." And he concludes, "Therefore, all gifts, virtues, and graces are dispensed through her hands

---

[38] *De Laud. B. M. V.*
[39] *De Cor. Virg.* c. 15.
[40] *De zona Deip.*
[41] *De Nativ.* s. i.
[42] P. 4, tit. 15, c. 22.

to whom she wills, and as she wills."[43] St. Bonaventure says the same: "Since the whole divine nature was in the womb of the Virgin, I do not fear to teach that she has a certain jurisdiction over all the streams of grace; as her womb was, as it were, an ocean of the divine nature, whence all the streams of grace must emanate." On the authority of these saints, many theologians have piously and reasonably defended the opinion that there is no grace given to us except by means of the intercession of Mary; so Mendoza, Vega, Paciucchelli, Segneri, Piore, Crasset, and others, as also the learned Alexander Natalis, who says: "It is God's will that we should look to Him for all good things, to be procured by the most powerful intercession of the Blessed Virgin, when we invoke her, as it is fit."[44] And he quotes in confirmation the passage of St. Bernard: "Such is His will, who has determined that we should receive all through Mary."[45] Contenson says the same, in a comment on the words addressed by Jesus on the Cross to St. John: "Behold thy Mother" (John 19:27), as though he had said, "No one shall be partaker of my blood except by the intercession of my Mother. My wounds are fountains of grace; but their streams shall flow to no one, except through the canal of Mary. O my disciple John, I will love you as you love her!"[46]

For the rest, it is certain that if God is pleased when we have recourse to the saints, He will be much more pleased when we avail ourselves of the intercession of Mary, that she, by her merits, may compensate for our unworthiness, according to the words of St. Anselm: "That the dignity of the intercessor may supply for

---

[43] *S. d. Nat. M. V.* c. 8.
[44] Ep. 50, in calce Theol.
[45] *De Aquoed.*
[46] *Theol. ment. et cord.* t. 2, 1. 10, d. 4, c. I.

our poverty. So that, to invoke the Virgin is not to distrust God's mercy, but to fear our own unworthiness."[47] St. Thomas, speaking of her dignity, calls it, as it were, infinite: "From the fact that she is the Mother of God, she has a certain infinite dignity."[48] So that it may be said with reason that the prayers of Mary have more power with God than those of all Heaven together.

Conclusion of the Chapter

Let us conclude this first point by giving the gist of all that has been said hitherto. He who prays is certainly saved. He who prays not is certainly damned. All the blessed (except infants) have been saved by prayer. All the damned have been lost through not praying; if they had prayed, they would not have been lost. And this is, and will be, their greatest torment in Hell, to think how easily they might have been saved, only by asking God for His grace; but that now it is too late — the time of prayer is over.

---

[47] *De incarn.* q. 37, a. 4, d. 23, s. 3.
[48] P. I, q. 25, a. 6. ad 4.

Chapter 2

••• ◁•●•▷ •••

The Power of Prayer

1. The Excellence of Prayer and Its Power with God

Our prayers are so dear to God that He has appointed the angels to present them to Him as soon as they come forth from our mouths. "The angels," says St. Hilary, "preside over the prayers of the faithful and offer them daily to God." This is that smoke of the incense, which are the prayers of saints, which St. John saw ascending to God from the hands of the angels (Rev. 8:3); and which he saw in another place represented by golden phials full of sweet odors, very acceptable to God. But in order to understand better the value of prayers in God's sight, it is sufficient to read both in the Old and New Testaments the innumerable promises which God makes to the man who prays. "Cry to me, and I will hear you" (Ps. 49:15). "Call upon me, and I will deliver you" (Jer. 33:3). "Ask, and it shall be given you; seek, and you shall find; knock, and it shall be opened to you. He shall give good things to them that ask Him" (Matt. 7:7). "Everyone that asks receives, and he that seeks finds" (Luke 11:10). "Whatsoever they shall ask, it shall be done for them by my Father" (John 15:7). "All things whatsoever you ask when you pray, believe that you shall receive them, and they shall come to you" (Matt. 18:19). "If you ask me anything in my name, that will I do" (John 14:14). "You shall ask whatever you will, and it shall be done to you. Amen, amen, I say to you, if you ask the Father anything in my name, He will give it to you" (John 16:23). There are a thousand similar texts; but it would take too long to quote them.

God wills us to be saved; but for our greater good, He wills us to be saved as conquerors. While, therefore, we remain here, we have to live in a continual warfare; and if we should be saved, we have to fight and conquer. "No one can be crowned without victory," says St. Chrysostom.[49] We are very feeble, and our enemies are many and mighty; how shall we be able to stand against them or to defeat them? Let us take courage and say with the apostle, "I can do all things in Him who strengthens me" (Phil. 4:13). By prayer we can do all things; for by this means, God will give us that strength which we want. Theodoret says that prayer is omnipotent; it is but one, yet it can do all things: "Though prayer is one, it can do all things."[50] And St. Bonaventure asserts that by prayer we obtain every good and escape every evil: "By it is obtained the gain of every good and liberation from every evil."[51] St. Laurence Justinian says that by means of prayer we build for ourselves a strong tower, where we shall be secure from all the snares and assaults of our enemies: "By the exercise of prayer man is able to erect a citadel for himself."[52] "The powers of Hell are mighty," says St. Bernard, "but prayer is stronger than all the devils."[53] Yes, for by prayer the soul obtains God's help, which is

[49] *De Mart*, s. I.
[50] *Ap. Rodrig*. p. I, tr. 5, c. 14.
[51] *In Luc*. II.
[52] *De Cast. Conn.* c. 22.
[53] *De Modo bene viv.* s. 49.

stronger than any created power. Thus David encouraged himself in his alarms: "Praising I will call upon the Lord, and I shall be saved from my enemies" (Ps. 17:3). For, as St. Chrysostom says, "Prayer is a strong weapon, a defense, a port, and a treasure."[54] It is a weapon sufficient to overcome every assault of the devil; it is a defense to preserve us in every danger; it is a port where we may be safe in every tempest; and it is at the same time a treasure which provides us with every good.

2. The Power of Prayer against Temptation

God knows the great good which it does us to be obliged to pray and therefore permits us (as we have already shown in the previous chapter) to be assaulted by our enemies, in order that we may ask Him for the help which He offers and promises to us. But as He is pleased when we run to Him in our dangers, so is He displeased when He sees us neglectful of prayer. "As the king," says St. Bonaventure, "would think it faithlessness in an officer, when his post was attacked, not to ask him for reinforcements, he would be reputed a traitor if he did not request help from the king";[55] so God thinks Himself betrayed by the man who, when he finds himself surrounded by temptations, does not run to Him for assistance. For He desires to help us and only waits to be asked and then gives abundant succor. This is strikingly shown by Isaias, when, on God's part, he told king Ahaz to ask some sign to assure himself of God's readiness to help him: "Ask thee a sign of the Lord thy God" (Isa. 7:11). The faithless king answered: I will not ask, and I will not tempt the Lord; for he trusted in his own power to overcome his enemies without God's

---

[54] *Hom. in Ps.* 145.
[55] *Diaeta sal.* t. 2. c. 5.

aid. And for this the prophet reproved him: Hear, therefore, O house of David; is it a small thing for you to be grievous to men, that you are grievous to my God also? Because that man is grievous and offensive to God who will not ask Him for the graces which He offers.

"Come to me, all you that labor and are burdened, and I will refresh you" (Matt. 11:28). "My poor children," says our Savior, "though you find yourselves assailed by enemies, and oppressed with the weight of your sins, do not lose heart but have recourse to me in prayer, and I will give you strength to resist, and I will give you a remedy for all your disasters." In another place He says by the mouth of Isaias, "Come and accuse me, says the Lord; if your sins be as scarlet, they shall be made white as snow" (Isa. 1:18). O men, come to me; though your consciences are horribly defiled, yet come; I even give you leave to reproach me (so to speak), if, after you have had recourse to me, I do not give you grace to become white as snow.

What is prayer? It is, as St. Chrysostom says, "the anchor of those tossed on the sea, the treasure of the poor, the cure of diseases, the safeguard of health."[56] It is a secure anchor for him who is in peril of shipwreck; it is a treasury of immense wealth for him who is poor; it is a most efficacious medicine for him who is sick; and it is a certain preservative for him who would keep himself well. What does prayer effect? Let us hear St. Laurence Justinian: "It pleases God, it gets what it asks, it overcomes enemies, it changes men."[57] It appeases the wrath of God, who pardons all who pray with humility. It obtains every grace that is asked for, it vanquishes all the strength of the tempter, and it changes

---

[56] *Hom. de Consubst. cont. Anom.*
[57] *De Perf.* c. 12.

men from blind into seeing, from weak into strong, from sinners into saints. Let him who wants light ask it of God, and it shall be given. "As soon as I had recourse to God," says Solomon, "He granted me wisdom: I called upon God, and the Spirit of wisdom came to me" (Wisd. 7:7). Let him who wants fortitude ask it of God, and it shall be given. "As soon as I opened my mouth to pray," says David, "I received help from God: I opened my mouth, and drew in the Spirit" (Ps. 118:131). And how in the world did the martyrs obtain strength to resist tyrants, except by prayer, which gave them force to overcome dangers and death?

"He who uses this great weapon," says St. Chrysostom, "knows not death, leaves the earth, enters Heaven, lives with God."[58] He falls not into sin; he loses affection for the earth; he makes his abode in Heaven and begins, even in this life, to enjoy the conversation of God. How then can you disquiet such a man by saying: "How do you know that you are written in the book of life?" How do you know whether God will give you efficacious grace and the gift of perseverance? "Be not solicitous," says St. Paul, "but in everything, by prayer and supplicatory, with thanksgiving, let your petitions be known to God" (Phil. 4:6). What is the use, says the apostle, of agitating yourselves with these miseries and fears? Drive from you all these cares, which are of no use but to lessen your confidence and to make you more tepid and slothful in walking along the way of salvation. Pray and seek always, and make your prayers sound in God's ears, and thank Him for having promised to give you the gifts which you desire whenever you ask for them, namely, efficacious grace, perseverance, salvation, and everything that you desire. The Lord has given us our post in the battle against powerful foes; but He is

---

[58] Sermon 45.

faithful in His promises and will never allow us to be assaulted more violently than we can resist: "God is faithful, who will not suffer you to be tempted above that which thou are able" (1 Cor. 10:13). He is faithful, since He instantly succors the man who invokes Him. The learned Cardinal Gotti writes that God has bound Himself not only to give us grace precisely balancing the temptation that assails us, but that He is obliged, when we are tempted, and have recourse to Him, to afford us, by means of that grace which is kept ready for and offered to all, sufficient strength for us actually to resist the temptation. "God is bound, when we are tempted, and fly to His protection, to give us by the grace prepared and offered to all such strength as will not only put us in the way of being able to resist, but will also make us resist; 'for we can do all things in Him who strengthens us' by His grace, if we humbly ask for it."[59] We can do all things with God's help, which is granted to everyone who humbly seeks it; so that we have no excuse when we allow ourselves to be overcome by a temptation. We are conquered solely by our own fault because we would not pray. By prayer, all the snares and power of the devil are easily overcome. "By prayer, all hurtful things are chased away," says St. Augustine.[60]

3. God Is Always Ready to Hear Us

St. Bernardine of Siena says that prayer is a faithful ambassador, well known to the King of Heaven, and having access to His private chamber, and able by His importunity to induce the merciful heart of the King to grant every aid to us, His wretched creatures, groaning in the midst of our conflicts and miseries in

[59] *De Grat.* q. 2. d. 5, § 3.
[60] *De Sal. Doc.* c. 28.

this valley of tears. "Prayer is a most faithful messenger, known to the King, who is used to enter His chamber, and by His importunity to influence the merciful mind of the King, and to obtain us assistance in our toils."[61] Isaias also assures us that as soon as the Lord hears our prayers, He is moved with compassion toward us and does not leave us to cry long to Him, but instantly replies and grants us what we ask: "Weeping, you shall not weep; He will surely have pity upon you: the voice of your cry as soon as He shall hear, He will answer you" (Isa. 30:19). In another place He complains of us by the mouth of Jeremias: "Am I become a wilderness to Israel, or a lateward springing land? Why then have my people said, we are revolted, and will come to you no more" (Jer. 2:31)? Why do you say that you will no more have recourse to me? Has my mercy become to you a barren land which can yield you no fruits of grace? Or a cold soil which yields its fruit too late? So has our loving Lord assured us that He never neglects to hear us and to hear us instantly when we pray; and so does He reproach those who neglect to pray through distrust of being heard.

If God were to allow us to present our petitions to Him once a month, even this would be a great favor. The kings of the earth give audiences a few times in the year, but God gives a continual audience. St. Chrysostom writes that God is always waiting to hear our prayers and that a case never occurred when He neglected to hear a petition offered to Him properly: "God is always prepared for the voice of His servants, nor did He ever, when called upon as He ought to be, neglect to hear."[62] And in another place, he says that when we pray to God, before we have

---

[61] T. 4. s. *in Dom.* 5. p. Pasc.
[62] *In Matt. hom.* 55.

finished recounting to Him our supplications, He has already heard us: "It is always obtained, even while we are yet praying." We even have the promise of God to do this: "As they are yet speaking I will hear" (Isa. 65:24). The Lord, says David, stands near to everyone who prays, to console, to hear, and to save him: The Lord is nigh to all them that call upon Him; to all that call upon Him in truth (that is, as they ought to call). "He will do the will of them that fear Him; and He will hear their prayer and will save them" (Ps. 144:18, 19). This it was in which Moses gloried, when he said: "There is not another nation so great, that has gods so nigh them, as our God is present to all our petitions "(Deut. 4:7). The gods of the Gentiles were deaf to those who invoked them, for they were wretched fabrications, which could do nothing. But our God, who is Almighty, is not deaf to our prayers, but always stands near the man who prays, ready to grant him all the graces which he asks: "In what day soever I shall call upon You, behold I shall know that You are my God" (Ps. 55:10). Lord, says the Psalmist, hereby do I know that You, my God, are all goodness and mercy, in that, whenever I have recourse to You, You instantly help me.

4. We Should Not Limit Ourselves to Asking for Little Things; To Pray Is Better Than to Meditate

We are so poor that we have nothing; but if we pray, we are no longer poor. If we are poor, God is rich; and God, as the apostle says, is all liberality to him that calls for His aid: "Rich unto all who call upon Him" (Rom. 10:12). Since, therefore (as St. Augustine exhorts us), we have to do with a Lord of infinite power and infinite riches, let us not go to Him for little and valueless things, but let us ask some great thing of Him: "You seek from the Almighty—seek something great."[63] If a man went to a king to ask some trumpery coin, like a farthing, I think that man would but insult his king. On the other hand, we honor God, we honor His mercy and His liberality, when, though we see how miserable we are, and how unworthy of any kindness, we yet ask for great graces, trusting in the goodness of God, and in His faithfulness to His promises of granting to the man who prays whatever grace he asks: "Whatsoever you will, ask, and it shall be done unto you" (John 15:7). St. Mary Magdalene of Pazzi said that "God feels Himself so honored and is so delighted when we ask for His grace, that He is, in a certain sense, grateful to us; because when we do this we seem to open to Him a way to do us a kindness, and to satisfy His nature, which is to do good to all." And let us be sure that, when we seek God's grace, He always gives us more than we ask. "If any of you want wisdom, let him ask of God, who gives to all abundantly, and upbraids not "(James 15). Thus speaks St. James, to show us that God is not like men, parsimonious of His goods; men, though rich and liberal, when they give alms, are always somewhat close-handed, and generally give less than is asked of them, because their wealth, however great it be, is always finite; so that the more they give, the less they have. But God, when He is asked, gives His good things "abundantly," that is, with a generous hand, always giving more than is asked, because His wealth is infinite, and the more He gives, the more He has to give: "For You, O Lord, are sweet and mild; and plenteous in mercy to all that call upon You" (Ps. 85:5). You, O my God, said David, are but too liberal and kind to him who invokes You; the mercies which You pour upon him are superabundant, above all he asks.

[63] *In Ps.* 62.

Prayer

On this point, then, we have to fix all our attention, namely, to pray with confidence, feeling sure that by prayer all the treasures of Heaven are thrown open to us. "Let us attend to this," says St. Chrysostom, "and we shall open Heaven to ourselves."[64] Prayer is a treasure; he who prays most receives most. St. Bonaventure says that every time a man has recourse to God by fervent prayer, he gains good things that are of more value than the whole world: "Any day a man gains more by devout prayer than the whole world is worth."[65] Some devout souls spend a great deal of time in reading and in meditating but pay but little attention to prayer. There is no doubt that spiritual reading and meditation on the eternal truths are very useful things, "but," says St. Augustine, "it is of much more use to pray." By reading and meditating we learn our duty; but by prayer we obtain the grace to do it. "It is better to pray than to read: by reading we know what we ought to do; by prayer we receive what we ask." What is the use of knowing our duty, and then not doing it, but to make us more guilty in God's sight? Read and meditate as we like, we shall never satisfy our obligations, unless we ask of God the grace to fulfill them.

And, therefore, as St. Isidore observes, the devil is never more busy to distract us with the thoughts of worldly cares than when he perceives us praying and asking God for grace: "Then mostly does the devil insinuate thoughts, when he sees a man praying."[66] And why? Because the enemy sees that at no other time do we gain so many treasures of Heavenly goods as when we pray. This is the chief fruit of mental prayer, to ask God

---

[64] *In Act. hom.* 36.
[65] *De Perf. vitae*, c. 5.
[66] *Sent.* 1. 3, c. 7.

for the graces which we need for perseverance and for eternal salvation; and chiefly for this reason it is that mental prayer is morally necessary for the soul, to enable it to preserve itself in the grace of God. For if a person does not remember in the time of meditation to ask for the help necessary for perseverance, he will not do so at any other time; for without meditation he will not think of asking for it and will not even think of the necessity of asking it. On the other hand, he who makes his meditation every day will easily see the needs of his soul, its dangers, and the necessity of his prayer; and so, he will pray and will obtain the graces which will enable him to persevere and save his soul. Fr. Segneri said of himself that when he began to meditate, he aimed rather at exciting affections than at making prayers. But when he came to know the necessity and the immense utility of prayer, he more and more applied himself, in his long mental prayer, to making petitions.

"As a young swallow, so will I cry," said the devout king Hezekias (Isa. 38:14). The young swallow does nothing but cry to its mother for help and for food; so should we all do, if we would preserve our life of grace. We should be always crying to God for aid to avoid the death of sin and to advance in His holy love. Fr. Rodriguez relates that the ancient Fathers, who were our first instructors in the spiritual life, held a conference to determine which was the exercise most useful and most necessary for eternal salvation; and they determined that it was to repeat over and over again the short prayer of David, "Incline unto my aid, O God!" (Ps. 69:1). "This," says Cassian "is what everyone ought to do who wishes to be saved: he ought to be always saying, My God, help me! My God, help me!" We ought to do this the first thing when we awake in the morning and then to continue doing it in all our needs, and when attending to our business, whether spiritual or temporal; and most especially when we find ourselves troubled by any temptation or passion. St. Bonaventure says that at times we obtain a grace by a short prayer sooner than by many other good works: "Sometimes a man can sooner obtain by a short prayer what he would be a long time obtaining by pious works."[67] St. Ambrose says that he who prays, while he is praying obtains what he asks, because the very act of prayer is the same as receiving: "He who asks of God, while he asks receives; for to ask is to receive." Hence St. Chrysostom wrote that "there is nothing more powerful than a man who prays,"[68] because such a one is made partaker of the power of God. To arrive at perfection, says St. Bernard, we must meditate and pray: by meditation we see what we want; by prayer we receive what we want. "Let us mount by meditation and prayer: the one teaches what is deficient, the other obtains that there should be nothing deficient."[69]

Conclusion of the Chapter

In conclusion, to save one's soul without prayer is most difficult, and even (as we have seen) impossible, according to the ordinary course of God's providence. But by praying, our salvation is made secure and very easy. It is not necessary in order to save our souls to go among the heathen and give up our life. It is not necessary to retire into the desert and eat nothing but herbs. What does it cost us to say, My God, help me! Lord, assist me! Have mercy on me! Is there anything more easy than this? And this little will suffice to save us, if we will be diligent in doing it. St. Laurence Justinian specially exhorts us to oblige ourselves to say a prayer

[67] *De Prof. rel.* 1. 2, c. 65.
[68] *In Matt. hom.* 58.
[69] *De S. And.* s. I.

at least when we begin any action: "We must endeavor to offer a prayer at least in the beginning of every work."[70] Cassian attests that the principal advice of the ancient Fathers was to have recourse to God with short but frequent prayers. Let no one, says St. Bernard, think lightly of prayer because God values it and then gives us either what we ask or what is still more useful to us: "Let no one undervalue his prayer, for God does not undervalue it.... He will give either what we ask, or what He knows to be better."[71] And let us understand that if we do not pray, we have no excuse, because the grace of prayer is given to everyone. It is in our power to pray whenever we will, as David says of himself: "With me is prayer to the God of my life; I will say to God, You are my support" (Ps. 41:8–9).

God gives to all the grace of prayer, in order that thereby they may obtain every help, and even more than they need, for keeping the divine law and for persevering till death. If we are not saved, the whole fault will be ours; and we shall have our own failure to answer for, because we did not pray.

---

[70] *Lign. vitae de or.* c. 6.
[71] *De Quad.* s. 5

Chapter 3

The Conditions of Prayer

1. Which Are the Requisite Conditions

Object of Prayer

"Amen, amen, I say to you, if you ask the Father anything in my name, He will give it you" (John 16:23). Jesus Christ then has promised that whatever we ask His Father in His name, His Father will give us. But always with the understanding that we ask under the proper conditions.

Many seek, says St. James, and obtain not because they seek improperly: "Ye ask and receive not, because ye ask amiss" (James 4:3). So St. Basil, following out the argument of the apostle, says, "You sometimes ask and receive not, because you have asked badly; either without faith, or you have requested things not fit for you, or you have not persevered";[72] "faithlessly," that is, with little faith, or little confidence; "lightly," with little desire of the grace you ask; "things not fit for you, when you seek good things that will not be conducive to your salvation; or you have left off praying, without perseverance."

---

[72] *Const. Mon.* c. i.

Prayer

Hence St. Thomas reduces to four the conditions required in prayer, in order that it may produce its effect: these are, that a man asks (1) for himself; (2) things necessary for salvation; (3) piously; and (4) with perseverance" (II-II, q. 83, art. 15).

Can We Pray Efficaciously for Others?

The first condition, then, of prayer is that you make it "for yourself" because St. Thomas holds that one man cannot "*ex condign*" (i.e. in the fitness of things) obtain for another eternal life; nor, consequently, even those graces which are requisite for his salvation, since, as he says, the promise is made not to others, but only to those that pray: "He shall give to you."

Nevertheless, there are many theologians, Cornelius a Lapide, Sylvester, Tolet, Habert, and others, who hold the opposite doctrine, on the authority of St. Basil, who teaches that prayer, by virtue of God's promise, is infallibly efficacious, even for those for whom we pray, provided they put no positive impediment in the way. And they support their doctrine by Scripture: "Pray one for another, that you may be saved; for the continual prayer of the just man availeth much" (James 5:16). "Pray for them that persecute and calumniate you" (Luke 6:28).

And better still, on the text of St. John: "He that knoweth his brother to sin a sin which is not to death, let him ask, and life shall be given to him who sinneth and not unto death. There is a sin unto death; for that I say not that any man ask" (1 John 5:16). St. Ambrose, St. Augustine, the Venerable Bede, and others (Apud. Calm. in loc. cit.) explain the words "who sinneth not unto death" to mean, provided the sinner is not one who intends to remain obstinate till death; since for such a one, a very extraordinary grace would be required. But for other sinners who are not guilty of such malice, the Apostle promises their conversion to him who prays for them: "Let him ask, and life shall be given him for him that sinneth."

We Ought to Pray for Sinners

Besides, it is quite certain that the prayers of others are of great use to sinners and are very pleasing to God; and God complains of His servants who do not recommend sinners to Him, as he once complained to St. Mary Magdalene of Pazzi, to whom He said one day: "See, my daughter, how the Christians are in the devil's hands; if my elect did not deliver them by their prayers, they would be devoured."

But God especially requires this of priests and religious. The same saint used to say to her nuns: "My sisters, God has not separated us from the world that we should only do good for ourselves, but also that we should appease Him on behalf of sinners"; and God one day said to her, "I have given to you, my chosen spouses, the City of Refuge (i.e., the Passion of Jesus Christ), that you may have a place where you may obtain help for my creatures. Therefore, have recourse to it, and thence stretch forth a helping hand to my creatures who are perishing, and lay down your lives for them."

For this reason, the saint, inflamed with holy zeal, used to offer God the Blood of the Redeemer fifty times a day on behalf of sinners and was quite wasted away for the desire she had for their conversion. Oh, she used to say, what pain is it, O Lord, to see how one could help Thy creatures by giving one's life for them, and not be able to do so! For the rest, in every exercise she recommended sinners to God; and it is written in her life that she scarcely passed an hour in the day without praying for them. Frequently, too, she arose in the middle of the night and went to the Blessed Sacrament to pray for them; and yet for all this, when she was once found bathed in tears, on being asked the cause, she answered, "Because I seem to myself to do nothing for the salvation of sinners." She went so far as to offer to endure even the pains of Hell for their conversion, provided that in that place she might still love God; and often God gratified her by inflicting on her grievous pains and infirmities for the salvation of sinners. She prayed especially for priests, seeing that their good life was the occasion of salvation to others, while their bad life was the cause of ruin to many; and therefore she prayed God to visit their faults upon her, saying, "Lord, make me die and return to life again as many times as is necessary to satisfy Thy justice for them!" And it is related in her life that the saint, by her prayers, did indeed release many souls from the hands of Lucifer.

I wished to speak rather particularly of the zeal of this saint; but, indeed, no souls who really love God neglect to pray for poor sinners. For how it is possible for a person who loves God, and knows what love He has for our souls, and what Jesus Christ has done and suffered for their salvation, and how our Savior desires us to pray for sinners, how is it possible, I say, that he should be able to look with indifference on the numbers of poor souls who are living without God, and are slaves of Hell, without being moved to importune God with frequent prayers to give light and strength to these wretched beings, so that they may come out from the miserable state of living death in which they are slumbering?

True it is that God has not promised to grant our requests, when those for whom we pray put a positive impediment in the way of their conversion; but still, God, in His goodness, has often deigned, at the prayer of His servants, to bring back the most blinded and obstinate sinners to a state of salvation, by means of extraordinary graces.

Therefore, let us never omit, when we say or hear Mass, when we receive Holy Communion, when we make our meditation or our visit to the Blessed Sacrament, to recommend poor sinners to God. And a learned author says that he who prays for others will find that his prayers for himself are heard much sooner. But this is a digression. Let us now return to the examination of the other conditions that St. Thomas lays down as necessary to the efficacy of prayer.

We Must Ask for the Graces Necessary to Salvation

The second condition assigned by the saint is that we ask those favors which are necessary to salvation; because the promise annexed to prayer was not made with reference to temporal favors, which are not necessary for the salvation of the soul.

St. Augustine, explaining the words of the Gospel "Whatever ye shall ask in my name" says that "nothing which is asked in a way detrimental to salvation is asked in the name of the Savior."[73] Sometimes, says the same Father, we seek some temporal favors, and God does not hear us; but He does not hear us because He loves us and wishes to be merciful to us. "A man may pray faithfully for the necessities of this life, and God may mercifully refuse to hear him; because the physician knows better than the patient what is good for the sick man."[74]

The physician who loves his patient will not allow him to have those things that he sees would do him harm. Oh, how many, if they had been sick or poor, would have escaped those sins which they commit in health and in affluence! And, therefore, when men ask God for health or riches, He often denies them

---

[73] *In Jo.* tr. 102.
[74] *Ap. s. Prosp. Sent.* 212.

because He loves them, knowing that these things would be to them an occasion of losing His grace, or at any rate of growing tepid in the spiritual life. Not that we mean to say that it is any defect to pray to God for the necessaries of this present life, so far as they are not inconsistent with our eternal salvation, as the Wise Man said: "Give me only the necessaries of life" (Prov. 30:8). Nor is it a defect, says St. Thomas, (II-II q. 83, art. 6) to have an anxiety about such goods, if it is not inordinate.

The defect consists in desiring and seeking these temporal goods, and in having an inordinate anxiety about them, as if they were our highest good. Therefore, when we ask of God these temporal favors, we ought always to ask them with resignation, and with the condition if they will be useful to our souls; and when we see that God does not grant them, let us be certain that He then denies them to us for the love He bears us, and because He sees that they would be injurious to the salvation of our souls. It often happens that we pray God to deliver us from some dangerous temptation, and yet that God does not hear us but permits the temptation to continue troubling us. In such a case, let us understand that God permits even this for our greater good. It is not temptation or bad thoughts that separate us from God, but our consent to the evil.

When a soul in temptation recommends itself to God, and by His aid resists, oh, how it then advances in perfection and unites itself more closely to God! And this is the reason why God does not hear it. St. Paul prayed instantly to be delivered from the temptation of impurity: "There was given me a sting of my flesh, an angel of Satan to buffet me; for which thing thrice I besought the Lord, that it might depart from me" (2 Cor. 12:7). But God answered him that it was enough to have His grace: "My grace is sufficient for thee." So that even in temptations we ought to pray with resignation, saying, Lord, deliver me from this trouble, if it is expedient to deliver me; and if not, at least give me help to resist.

And here comes in what St. Bernard says, that when we beg any grace of God, He gives us either that which we ask or some other thing more useful to us. He often leaves us to be buffeted by the waves in order to try our faithfulness and for our greater profit. It seems then that He is deaf to our prayers. But no; let us be sure that God then really hears us, and secretly aids us, and strengthens us by His grace to resist all the assaults of our enemies. See how He Himself assures us of this by the mouth of the psalmist: "Thou calledst upon me in affliction, and I delivered thee: I heard thee in the secret place of tempest; I proved thee at the waters of contradiction" (Ps. 80:8).

Other Conditions of Prayer

The other conditions assigned by St. Thomas to prayer are that it is to be made piously and perseveringly: by piously, he means with humility and confidence; by perseveringly, continuing to pray until death. We must now speak distinctly of each of these three conditions, which are the most necessary for prayer, namely, of humility, confidence, and perseverance.

2. The Humility with Which We Should Pray

The Lord does indeed regard the prayers of His servants, but only of His servants who are humble. "He hath had regard to the prayer of the humble" (Ps. 101:18). Others He does not regard but rejects them: "God resisteth the proud and giveth grace to the humble" (James 4:6). He does not hear the prayers of the proud who trust in their own strength but, for that reason, leaves them to their own feebleness; and in this state, deprived of God's aid, they must certainly perish. David had to bewail this case: "Before I was humbled, I offended" (Ps. 118:67). I sinned because I was not humble.

The same thing happened to St. Peter, who, though he was warned by Our Lord that all the disciples would abandon Him on that night—"All you shall be scandalized in me this night" (Matt. 26:31)—nevertheless, instead of acknowledging his own weakness, and begging Our Lord's aid against his unfaithfulness, was too confident in his own strength and said that, though all should abandon Him, he would never leave Him: "Although all shall be scandalized in Thee, I will never be scandalized." And although our Savior again foretold to him, in a special manner, that in that very night, before the cock-crow, he should deny Him three times; yet, trusting in his own courage, he boasted, saying, "Yea, though I should die with Thee, I will not deny Thee." But what came of it? Scarcely had the unhappy man entered the house of the high priest when he was accused of being a disciple of Jesus Christ, and three times did he deny with an oath that he had ever known Him: "And again he denied with an oath, that I know not the Man." If Peter had humbled himself and had asked Our Lord for the grace of constancy, he would not have denied Him.

We ought all to feel that we are standing on the edge of a precipice, suspended over the abyss of all sins, and supported only by the thread of God's grace. If this thread fails us, we shall certainly fall into the gulf and shall commit the most horrible wickedness. "Unless the Lord had been my helper, my soul had almost dwelt in Hell" (Ps. 93:17). If God had not succored me, I should have fallen into a thousand sins, and now I should be in Hell. So said the psalmist, and so ought each of us to say. This is what St. Francis of Assisi meant when he said that he was the worst sinner in the world. But, my Father, said his companion, what you say is not true; there are many in the world who are certainly worse than you are. Yes, what I say is but too true, answered St. Francis; because if God did not keep His hand over me, I should commit every possible sin.

It is of faith that, without the aid of grace, we cannot do any good work nor even think a good thought. "Without grace men do no good whatever, either in thought or in deed," says St. Augustine.[75] As the eye cannot see without light, so, says the holy Father, man can do not good without grace. The Apostle had said the same thing before him: "Not that we are sufficient to think anything of ourselves, as of ourselves; but our sufficiency is of God" (2 Cor. 3:5). And David had said it before St. Paul: "Unless the Lord build the house, they labor in vain that build it" (Ps. 126:1).

In vain does man weary himself to become a saint, unless God lends a helping hand: "Unless the Lord keep the city, he watcheth in vain that keepeth it." If God did not preserve the soul from sins, in vain will it try to preserve itself by its own strength: and therefore did the holy prophet protest, "I will not trust in my bow" (Ps. 43:7). I will not hope in my arms; but only in God, who alone can save me.

Hence, whoever finds that he has done any good and does not find that he has fallen into greater sins than those which are commonly committed, let him say with St. Paul, "By the grace of God I am what I am" (1 Cor. 15:10) and for the same reason, he ought never to cease to be afraid of falling on every occasion of sin: "Wherefore, he that thinketh himself to stand, let him take heed lest he fall" (1 Cor. 10:12). St. Paul wishes to warn us that he who feels secure of not falling is in great danger of falling; and he assigns the reason in another place, where he

---

[75] *De Corr. et Gr.* c. 2.

says, "If any man think himself to be something, whereas he is nothing, he deceiveth himself" (Gal. 6:3).

So that St. Augustine wrote wisely, "The presumption of stability renders many unstable; no one will be so firm as he who feels himself infirm."[76] If a man says he has no fear, it is a sign that he trusts in himself and in his good resolutions; but such a man, with his mischievous confidence, deceives himself, because, through trust in his own strength, he neglects to fear; and through not fearing, he neglects to recommend himself to God, and then he will certainly fall.

And so, for like reasons, we should all abstain from noticing with any vainglory the sins of other people; but rather we should then esteem ourselves as worse in ourselves than they are and should say, Lord, if Thou hadst not helped, I should have done worse. Otherwise, to punish us for our pride, God will permit us to fall into worse and more shameful sins.

For this cause St. Paul instructs us to labor for our salvation. But how? Always in fear and trembling: "With fear and trembling work out your salvation" (Phil. 2:12). Yes, for he who has a great fear of falling distrusts his own strength and therefore places his confidence in God and will have recourse to Him in dangers; and God will aid him, and so he will vanquish his temptations and will be saved. St. Philip Neri, walking one day through Rome, kept saying, "I am in despair!" A certain religious rebuked him, and the saint thereupon said, "My father, I am in despair for myself; but I trust in God."

So must we do, if we would be saved; we must always live in despair of doing anything by our own strength; and in so doing we shall imitate St. Philip, who used to say to God the first

[76] Sermon 76 E. B.

moment he woke in the morning, "Lord, keep Thy hands over Philip this day; for if not, Philip will betray Thee."

This, then, we may conclude with St. Augustine, is all the grand science of a Christian, to know that he is nothing and can do nothing. "This is the whole of the great science, to know that man is nothing."[77] For then he will never neglect to furnish himself, by prayer to God, with that strength which he has not of himself and which he needs in order to resist temptation and to do good; and so, with the help of God, who never refuses anything to the man who prays to Him in humility, he will be able to do all things: "The prayer of him that humbleth himself shall pierce the clouds, and he will not depart until the Most High behold" (Eccles. 35:21).

The prayer of a humble soul penetrates the heavens, and presents itself before the throne of God, and departs not without God's looking on it and hearing it. And though the soul be guilty of any amount of sin, God never despises a heart that humbles itself: "A contrite and humble heart, O God, Thou wilt not despise (Ps. 1:19); God resisteth the proud, but giveth grace to the humble" (James 4:6). As the Lord is severe with the proud and resists their prayers, so is He kind and liberal to the humble. This is precisely what Jesus Christ said one day to St. Catherine of Siena: "Know, my daughter, that a soul that perseveres in humble prayer gains every virtue."[78]

It will be of use to introduce here the advice which the learned and pious Palafox, bishop of Osma, gives to spiritual persons who desire to become saints. It occurs in a note to the eighteenth letter of St. Teresa, which she wrote to her Confessor, to give him an account of all the grades of supernatural prayer with which God

---

[77] *In Ps.* 70, S. 1.
[78] *Ap. Blos, in Concl.* p. 2, c. 3.

had favored her. On this the bishop writes, that these supernatural graces which God deigned to grant to St. Teresa, as He has also done to other saints, are not necessary in order to arrive at sanctity, since many souls have become saints without them; and, on the other hand, many have arrived at sanctity and yet have, after all, been damned. Therefore, he says, it is superfluous, and even presumptuous, to desire and to ask for these supernatural gifts, when the true and only way to become a saint is to exercise ourselves in virtue and in the love of God; and this is done by means of prayer and by corresponding to the inspirations and assistance of God, who wishes nothing so much as to see us saints. "For this is the will of God, your sanctification" (1 Thess. 4:3).

Hence Bishop Palafox, speaking of the grades of supernatural prayer mentioned in St. Teresa's letter — namely, the prayer of quiet, the sleep or suspension of the faculties, the prayer of union, ecstasy or rapture, flight and impulse of the spirit, and the wound of love — says very wisely that, as regards the prayer of quiet, what we ought to ask of God is that He would free us from attachment to worldly goods and the desire of them, which give no peace but bring disquiet and affliction to the soul: "Vanity of vanities," as Solomon well called them, "and vexation of spirit" (Eccles. 1:14). The heart of man will never find true peace if it does not empty itself of all that is not God, so as to leave itself all free for His love, that He alone may possess the whole of it. But this the soul cannot do of itself; it must obtain it of God by repeated prayers.

As regards "the sleep and suspension of the faculties," we ought to ask God for grace to keep them asleep for all that is temporal and only awaken them to consider God's goodness, and to set our hearts upon His love and eternal happiness.

As regards the "union of the faculties," let us pray Him to give us grace not to think, nor to seek, nor to wish anything but what

God wills; since all sanctity and the perfection of love consists in uniting our will to the will of God.

As regards "ecstasy and rapture," let us pray God to draw us away from the inordinate love of ourselves and of creatures and to draw us entirely to Himself.

As regards "the flight of the spirit," let us pray Him to give us grace to live altogether detached from this world and to do as the swallows, which do not settle on the ground even to feed but take their food flying; so should we use our temporal goods for all that is necessary for the support of life, but always flying, without settling on the ground to look for earthly pleasures.

As regards "impulse of spirit," let us pray Him to give us courage and strength to do violence to ourselves, whenever it is necessary, for resisting the assaults of our enemies, for conquering our passions, and for accepting sufferings even in the midst of desolation and dryness of spirit.

Finally, as regards "the wound of love," as a wound, by its pain, perpetually renews the remembrance of what we suffer, so ought we to pray God to wound our hearts with His holy love in such a way that we shall always be reminded of His goodness and the love which He has borne us; and thus we should live in continual love of Him and should be always pleasing Him with our works and our affections. But none of these graces can be obtained without prayer; and with prayer, provided it be humble, confident, and persevering, everything is obtained.

3. The Confidence with Which We Ought to Pray

Excellence and Necessity of This Virtue

The principal instruction that St. James gives us, if we wish by prayer to obtain grace from God, is that we pray with a confidence that feels sure of being heard, and with out hesitating: "Let him ask in faith, nothing wavering" (James 1:6).

St. Thomas teaches that as prayer receives its power of meriting from charity, so, on the other hand, it receives from faith and confidence its power of being efficacious to obtain: "Prayer has its power of meriting from charity, but its efficacy of obtaining from faith and confidence" (II-II, q. 83, art. 15). St. Bernard teaches the same, saying that it is our confidence alone which obtains for us the divine mercies: "Hope alone obtains a place of mercy with Thee, O Lord."[79]

God is much pleased with our confidence in His mercy because we then honor and exalt that infinite goodness which it was His object in creating us to manifest to the world: "Let all those, O my God," says the royal prophet, who hope in Thee be glad, for they shall be eternally happy, and Thou shalt dwell in them" (Ps. 5:12). God protects and saves all those who confide in Him: "He is the Protector of all that hope in Him" (Ps. 17:31). "Thou who savest them that trust in Thee" (Ps. 16:7).

Oh, the great promises that are recorded in the Scriptures to all those who hope in God! He who hopes in God will not fall into sin: "None of them that trust in Him shall offend" (Ps. 33:23). Yes, says David, because God has His eyes turned to all those who confide in His goodness to deliver them by His aid from the death of sin. "Behold, the eyes of the Lord are on them that fear Him, and on them that hope for His mercy to deliver their souls from death" (Ps. 32:18). And in another place God Himself says: "Because he hoped in me I will deliver him; I will protect him; I will deliver him and I will glorify him" (Ps. 90:14). Mark the word "because." "Because" he confided in me, I will protect

[79] *De Annunt.* s. 3.

him; I will deliver him from his enemies and from the danger of falling; and finally I will give him eternal glory.

Isaias says of those who place their hope in God: "They that hope in the Lord shall renew their strength; they shall take wings as the eagles; they shall run and not be weary: they shall walk and not faint" (Isa. 40:31). They shall cease to be weak, as they are now, and shall gain in God a great strength; they shall not faint; they shall not even feel weary in walking the way of salvation, but they shall run and fly as eagles; "in silence and in hope shall your strength be" (Isa. 30:15). All our strength, the prophet tells us, consists in placing all our confidence in God, and in being silent; that is, in reposing in the arms of His mercy, without trusting to our own efforts, or to human means.

And when did it ever happen that a man had confidence in God and was lost? "No one hath hoped in the Lord and hath been confounded" (Eccles. 2:11). It was this confidence that assured David that he should not perish: "In Thee, O Lord, have I trusted; I shall not be confounded forever" (Ps. 30:2). Perhaps, then, says St. Augustine, God could be a deceiver, who offers to support us in dangers if we lean upon Him, and would then withdraw Himself if we had recourse to Him? "God is not a deceiver, that He should offer to support us, and then when we lean upon Him should slip away from us."[80] David calls the man happy who trusts in God: "Blessed is the man that trusteth in Thee" (Ps. 83:13). And why? Because, says he, he who trusts in God will always find himself surrounded by God's mercy. "Mercy shall encompass him that hopeth in the Lord" (Ps. 31:10). So that he shall be surrounded and guarded by God on every side in such a way that he shall be prevented from losing his soul.

[80] *Thomas. Erud. Princ.* 1. 2, c. 5

Prayer

It is for this cause that the Apostle recommends us so earnestly to preserve our confidence in God; for (he tells us) it will certainly obtain from Him a great remuneration: "Do not therefore lose your confidence, which hath a great reward" (Heb. 10:35). As in our confidence, so shall be the graces we receive from God: if our confidence is great, great too will be the graces: "Great faith merits great things."[81]

St. Bernard writes that the divine mercy is an inexhaustible fountain and that he who brings to it the largest vessel of confidence shall take from it the largest measure of gifts: "Neither, O Lord, dost Thou put the oil of Thy mercy into any other vessel than that of confidence."[82] The prophet had long before expressed the same thought: "Let Thy mercy, O Lord, be upon us [i.e., in proportion] as we have hoped in Thee" (Ps. 32:22). This was well exemplified in the centurion to whom our Savior said, in praise of his confidence, "Go, and as thou hast believed, so be it done unto thee" (Matt. 8:12). And Our Lord revealed to St. Gertrude that he who prays with confidence does Him in a manner such violence that He cannot but hear him in everything he asks: "Prayer," says St. John Climacus, "does a pious violence to God." It does Him a violence, but a violence which He likes and which pleases Him.

"Let us go, therefore," according to the admonition of St. Paul, "with confidence to the throne of grace, that we may obtain mercy, and find grace in seasonable aid" (Heb. 4:16). The throne of grace is Jesus Christ, who is now sitting on the right hand of the Father; not on the throne of justice, but of grace, to obtain pardon for us if we fall into sin and help to enable us to persevere if we are enjoying His friendship.

[81] *In Cant.* s. 32.
[82] *De Annunt.* s. 3.

To this throne we must always have recourse with confidence; that is to say, with that trust which springs from faith in the goodness and truth of God, who has promised to hear him who prays to Him with confidence, but with a confidence that is both sure and stable.

On the other hand, says St. James, let not the man who prays with hesitation think that he will receive anything: "For he who wavereth is like a wave of the sea, which is moved and carried about by the wind. Therefore let not that man think to receive anything of the Lord" (James 1:6). He will receive nothing, because the diffidence which agitates him is unjust toward God and will hinder His mercy from listening to his prayers: "Thou hast not asked rightly, because thou hast asked doubtingly," says St. Basil; "thou hast not received grace, because thou hast asked it without confidence."[83]

David says that our confidence in God ought to be as firm as a mountain, which is not moved by each gust of wind. "They who trust in the Lord are as Mount Sion; he shall not be moved forever" (Ps. 124:1). And it is this that Our Lord recommends to us, if we wish to obtain the graces which we ask: "Whatsoever you ask when you pray, believe that you shall receive, and they shall come unto you" (Mark 11:24). Whatever grace you require, be sure of having it, and so you shall obtain it.

Foundation of Our Confidence

But on what, a man will say, am I, a miserable sinner, to found this certain confidence of obtaining what I ask? On what? On the promise made by Jesus Christ: "Ask, and you shall receive" (John 16:24). "Who will fear to be deceived, when the truth

---

[83] *Const. mon.* c. 2.

promises?" says St. Augustine.[84] How can we doubt that we shall be heard when God, who is truth itself, promises to give us that which we ask of Him in prayer? "We should not be exhorted to ask," says the same Father, "unless He meant to give."[85]

Certainly God would not have exhorted us to ask Him for favors if He had not determined to grant them; but this is the very thing to which He exhorts us so strongly and which is repeated so often in the Scriptures: pray, ask, seek, and you shall obtain what you desire: "Whatever you will, seek and it shall be done to you" (John 15:7). And in order that we may pray to Him with due confidence, our Savior has taught us, in the Our Father, that when we have recourse to Him for the graces necessary to salvation (all of which are included in the petitions of the Lord's Prayer), we should call Him, not Lord, but Father — "Our Father" — because it is His will that we should ask God for grace with the same confidence with which a son, when in want or sick, asks food or medicine from his own father.

If a son is dying of hunger, he has only to make his case known to his father, and his father will forthwith provide him with food; and if he has received a bite from a venomous serpent, he has only to show his father the wound, and the father will immediately apply whatever remedy he has.

Trusting, therefore, in God's promises, let us always pray with confidence; not vacillating, but stable and firm, as the Apostle says: "Let us hold fast the confession of our hope without wavering; for He is faithful that hath promised" (Heb. 10:23). As it is perfectly certain that God is faithful in His promises, so ought our faith also to be perfectly certain that He will hear us when we

---

[84] *Conf.* 1. 12, c. I.
[85] Sermon 105, E. B.

pray. And although sometimes, when we are in a state of aridity, or disturbed by some fault we have committed, we perhaps do not feel while praying that sensible confidence which we would wish to experience, yet, for all this, let us force ourselves to pray, and to pray without ceasing; for God will not neglect to hear us. Nay, rather, He will hear us more readily because we shall then pray with more distrust of ourselves and confiding only in the goodness and faithfulness of God, who has promised to hear the man who prays to Him. Oh, how God is pleased, in the time of our tribulations, of our fears, and of our temptations, to see us hope against hope; that is, in spite of the feeling of diffidence which we then experience because of our desolation! This is that for which the Apostle praises the patriarch Abraham, "who against hope, believed in hope" (Rom. 4:18).

St. John says that he who reposes a sure trust in God certainly will become a saint: "And every one that hath this hope in Him sanctifieth himself, as He also is holy" (1 John 3:3). For God gives abundant graces to them that trust in Him. By this confidence the host of martyrs, of virgins, even of children, in spite of the dread of the torments which their persecutors prepared for them, overcame both their tortures and their persecutors. Sometimes, I say, we pray, but it seems to us that God will not hear us. Alas!

Let us not then neglect to persevere in prayer and in hope; let us then say, with Job, "Although He should kill me, I will trust in Him" (Job 13:15). O my God! Though Thou hast driven me from Thy presence, I will not cease to pray and to hope in Thy mercy. Let us do so, and we shall obtain what we want from God. So did the Canaanite woman, and she obtained all that she wished from Jesus Christ. This woman had a daughter possessed by a devil, and prayed our Savior to deliver her: "Have mercy on me, my daughter is grievously tormented by a devil" (Matt. 15:22). Our Lord answered her that He was not sent for the Gentiles, of whom she was one, but for the Jews. She, however, did not lose heart but renewed her prayer with confidence: Lord, Thou canst console me! Thou must console me: "Lord, help me!" Jesus answered that, but as to the bread of the children, it is not good to give it to the dogs: "It is not good to take the children's bread, and to cast it to the dogs." But, my Lord, she answered, even the dogs are allowed to have the fragments of bread which fall from the table: "Yea, Lord; for the whelps eat of the crumbs that fall from the tables of their masters."

Then our Savior, seeing the great confidence of this woman, praised her and did what she asked, saying: "O woman, great is thy faith; be it done to thee as thou wilt." For who, says Ecclesiasticus, has ever called on God for aid and has been neglected and left unaided by Him? "Or who hath called upon Him, and He hath despised him?" (Ecclus. 2:12).

St. Augustine says that prayer is a key which opens Heaven to us; the same moment in which our prayer ascends to God, the grace which we ask for descends to us: "The prayer of the just is the key of Heaven; the petition ascends, and the mercy of God descends."[86] The royal prophet writes that our supplications and God's mercy are united together: "Blessed is God, who has not turned away my prayer, nor His mercy for me" (Ps. 65:20). And hence the same St. Augustine says that when we are praying to God, we ought to be certain that God is hearing us: "When you see that your prayer is not removed from you, be sure that His mercy is not removed from you."[87]

And for myself, I speak the truth, I never feel greater consolation, nor a greater confidence of my salvation, than when I am

---

[86] Sermon 47. E. B. app.
[87] *In Ps.* xv.

praying to God and recommending myself to Him. And I think that the same thing happens to all other believers; for the other signs of our salvation are uncertain and unstable; but that God hears the man who prays to Him with confidence is an infallible truth, as it is infallible that God cannot fail in His promises.

When we find ourselves weak and unable to overcome any passion, or any great difficulty, so as to fulfill that which God requires of us, let us take courage and say, with the Apostle, "I can do all things in Him, who strengtheneth me" (Phil. 4:13). Let us not say, as some do, I cannot; I distrust myself. With our own strength certainly we can do nothing; but with God's help we can do everything. If God said to anyone, "Take this mountain on your back and carry it, for I am helping you," would not the man be a mistrustful fool if he answered, "I will not take it; for I have not strength to carry it"? And thus, when we know how miserable and weak we are, and when we find ourselves most encompassed with temptations, let us not lose heart; but let us lift up our eyes to God and say, with David, "The Lord is my helper; and I will despise my enemies" (Ps. 117:7).

With the help of my Lord, I shall overcome and laugh to scorn all the assaults of my foes. And when we find ourselves in danger of offending God, or in any other critical position, and are too confused to know what is best to be done, let us recommend ourselves to God, saying, "The Lord is my light and my salvation; whom shall I fear?" (Ps. 26:1). And let us be sure that God will then certainly give us light and will save us from every evil.

The Prayer of Sinners

But I am a sinner, you will say; and in the Scriptures I read, "God heareth not sinners" (John 9:31). St. Thomas answers (with St. Augustine) that this was said by the blind man who, when he spoke, had not as yet been enlightened: "That is the word of a blind man not yet perfectly enlightened, and therefore it is not authoritative" (II-II, q. 83, art. 16). Though, adds St. Thomas, it is true of the petition which the sinner makes, "so far forth as he is a sinner"; that is, when he asks from a desire of continuing to sin — as, for instance, if he were to ask assistance to enable him to take revenge on his enemy or to execute any other bad intention. The same holds good for the sinner who prays God to save him but has no desire to quit the state of sin.

There are some unhappy persons who love the chains with which the devil keeps them bound like slaves. The prayers of such men are not heard by God because they are rash, presumptuous, and abominable. For what greater presumption can there be than for a man to ask favors of a prince whom he not only has often offended but whom he intends to offend still more? And this is the meaning of the Holy Spirit, when He says that the prayer of him who turns away his ears so as not to hear what God commands is detestable and odious to God: "He who turneth away his ears from learning the law, his prayer shall be an abomination" (Prov. 28:9).

To these people God says, it is of no use your praying to me, for I will turn my eyes from you and will not hear you: "When you stretch forth your hands, I will turn away my eyes from you; and when you multiply prayer, I will not hear" (Isa. 1:15). Such, precisely, was the prayer of the impious King Antiochus, who prayed to God and made great promises, but insincerely and with a heart obstinate in sin; the sole object of his prayer being to escape the punishment that impended over him; therefore, God did not hear his prayer but caused him to die devoured by worms: "Then this wicked man prayed to the Lord, of whom he was not to obtain mercy" (2 Macc. 9:13).

But others, who sin through frailty, or by the violence of some great passion, and who groan under the yoke of the enemy, and desire to break these chains of death, and to escape from their miserable slavery, and therefore ask the assistance of God; the prayer of these, if it is persevering, will certainly be heard by Him who says that every one who asks receives and he who seeks grace finds it: "For every one that asketh receiveth, and he that seeketh findeth" (Matt. 7:8). "Every one, whether he be a just man or a sinner," says the author of the *Opus Imperfectum.*[88]

And in St. Luke, Our Lord, when speaking of the man who gave all the loaves he had to his friend, not so much on account of his friendship as because of the other's importunity, says, "If he shall continue knocking, I say to you, although he will not rise and give him because he is his friend, yet because of his importunity he will rise and give him as many as he needeth" (Luke 11:8). "And so I say unto you, Ask, and it shall be given to you." So that persevering prayer obtains mercy from God, even for those who are not His friends.

That which is not obtained through friendship, says St. Chrysostom, is obtained by prayer: "That which was not effected by friendship was effected by prayer." He even says that prayer is valued more by God than friendship: "Friendship is not of such avail with God as prayer; that which is not effected by friendship is effected by prayer."[89] And St. Basil doubts not that even sinners obtain what they ask if they persevere in praying: "Sinners obtain what they seek, if they seek perseveringly."[90] St. Gregory says the same: "The sinner also shall cry, and his prayer shall

[88] Hom. 18.
[89] Hom. Non esse desp.
[90] *Const. Man.* c. I.

reach to God."[91] So St. Jerome, who says that even the sinner can call God his Father, if he prays to Him to receive him anew as a son; after the example of the prodigal son, who called Him Father, "Father, I have sinned" (Luke 15:21), even though he had not as yet been pardoned.

If God did not hear sinners, says St. Augustine, in vain would the publican have asked for forgiveness: "If God does not hear sinners, in vain would that publican have said, 'God be merciful to me a sinner.'"[92] But the Gospel assures us that the publican did by his prayer obtain forgiveness: "This man went down to his house justified" (Luke 18:14).

But further still, St. Thomas examines this point more minutely and does not hesitate to affirm that even the sinner is heard if he prays; for though his prayer is not meritorious, yet it has the power of impetration, that is, of obtaining what we ask; because impetration is not founded on God's justice but on His goodness. "Merit," he says, "depends on justice; impetration, on grace" (II-II, q. 83, art. 16). Thus did Daniel pray, "Incline, O my God, thine ear and hear ... for not in our justifications do we present our prayers before Thy face, but in the multitude of Thy mercies" (Dan. 9:18). Therefore, when we pray, says St. Thomas, it is not necessary to be friends of God in order to obtain the grace we ask; for prayer itself renders us His friends: "Prayer itself makes us of the family of God."[93]

Moreover, St. Bernard uses a beautiful explanation of this, saying that the prayer of a sinner to escape from sin arises from the desire to return to the grace of God. Now this desire is a gift,

[91] *In Ps.* vi. pan.
[92] *In Jo. tr.* 44.
[93] *Comp. Theol.* p.2 c.2.

which is certainly given by no other than God Himself; to what end, therefore, says St. Bernard, would God give to a sinner this holy desire, unless He meant to hear him? "For what would He give the desire, unless He willed to hear?" And, indeed, in the Holy Scriptures themselves there are multitudes of instances of sinners who have been delivered from sin by prayer. Thus was King Achab (3 Kings 21:27) delivered; thus King Manasses (2 Chron. 33:12); thus King Nabuchodonosor (Dan. 4:31); and thus the good thief (Luke 23:42). Oh, the wonderful! oh, the mighty power of prayer! Two sinners are dying on Calvary by the side of Jesus Christ: one, because he prays, "Remember me," is saved; the other, because he prays not, is damned.

And, in fine, St. Chrysostom says, "No man has with sorrow asked favors from Him without obtaining what he wished."[94] No sinner has ever with penitence prayed to God without having his desires granted. But why should we cite more authorities and give more reasons to demonstrate this point when Our Lord Himself says, "Come to me, all you that labor and are burdened, and I will refresh you" (Matt. 11:28). The "burdened," according to Sts. Augustine, Jerome, and others, are sinners in general who groan under the load of their sins and who, if they have recourse to God, will surely, according to His promise, be refreshed and saved by His grace.

Ah, we cannot desire to be pardoned as much as He longs to pardon us. "Thou dost not," says St. Chrysostom, "so much desire thy sins to be forgiven as He desires to forgive thy sins."[95] There is no grace, he goes on to say, that is not obtained by

[94] Hom. de Moys.
[95] *In Act.* hom. 36.

prayer, though it be the prayer of the most abandoned sinner, provided only it be persevering: "There is nothing which prayer cannot obtain, though a man be guilty of a thousand sins, provided it be fervent and unremitting." And let us mark well the words of St. James: "If any man wanteth wisdom, let him ask of God, who giveth to all abundantly, and upbraideth not" (James 1:5). All those, therefore, who pray to God, are infallibly heard by Him and receive grace in abundance: "He giveth to all abundantly." But you should particularly remark the words which follow: "and upbraideth not." This means that God does not do as men, who, when a person who has formerly done them an injury comes to ask a favor, immediately upbraid him with his offense. God does not do so to the man who prays, even though he were the greatest sinner in the world, when he asks for some grace conducive to his eternal salvation. Then He does not upbraid him with the offenses he has committed; but, as though he had never displeased Him, He instantly receives him, consoles him, hears him, and enriches him with an abundance of His gifts.

To crown all, our Savior, in order to encourage us to pray, says "Amen, amen, I say to you, if you ask the Father anything in my name, He will give it you" (John 16:23). As though He had said, "Courage, O sinners; do not despair: do not let your sins turn away from having recourse to my Father, and from hoping to be saved by Him, if you desire it. You have not now any merits to obtain the graces which you ask for, for you only deserve to be punished; still do this: go to my Father in my name, through my merits ask the favors which you want, and I promise and swear to you ("Amen amen, I say to you," which, according to St. Augustine, is a species of oath) that whatever you ask, my Father will grant." O God, what greater comfort can a sinner have after his fall than to know for certain that all he asks from God in the name of Jesus Christ will be given to him!

I say "all," but I mean only that which has reference to his eternal salvation; for with respect to temporal goods, we have already shown that God, even when asked, sometimes does not give them because He sees that they would injure our soul. But so far as relates to spiritual goods, His promise to hear us is not conditional but absolute; and therefore St. Augustine tells us that those things which God promises absolutely, we should demand with absolute certainty of receiving: "Those things which God promises, seek with certainty."[96] And how, says the saint, can God ever deny us His graces than we to receive them! "He is more willing to be munificent of His benefits to thee than thou art desirous to receive them."[97] St. Chrysostom says that the only time when God is angry with us is when we neglect to ask Him for his gifts: "He is only angry when we do not pray."[98] And how can it ever happen that God will not hear a soul who asks Him for favors all according to His pleasure? When the soul says to Him, Lord, I ask Thee not for goods of this world—riches, pleasures, honors; I ask Thee only for Thy grace: deliver me from sin, grant me a good death, give me Paradise, give me Thy holy love (which is that grace which St. Francis de Sales says we should seek more than all others), give me resignation to Thy will; how is it possible that God should not hear! What petitions wilt Thou, O my God, ever hear (says St. Augustine), if Thou dost not hear those which are made after Thy Own heart? "What prayers dost Thou hear, if Thou hearest not these?"[99]

<hr>

[96] Sermon 354, E. B.
[97] Sermon 105, E. B.
[98] *In Matt.* hom. 23.
[99] *De Civ. Dei*, 1, 22 c. 8.

But, above all, our confidence ought to revive, when we pray to God for spiritual graces, as Jesus Christ says: "If you, being evil, know how to give good gifts to your children, how much more will your Father from Heaven give the good Spirit to them that ask Him!" (Luke 11:13). If you, who are so attached to your own interests, so full of self-love, cannot refuse your children that which they ask, how much more will your Heavenly Father, who loves you better than any earthly father, grant you His spiritual goods when you pray for them!

4. The Perseverance Required in Prayer

Our prayers, then, must be humble and confident; but this is not enough to obtain final perseverance and thereby eternal life. Individual prayers will obtain the individual graces which they ask of God; but unless they are persevering, they will not obtain final perseverance, which, as it is the accumulation of many graces, requires many prayers, which are not to cease till death. The grace of salvation is not a single grace, but a chain of graces, all of which are at last linked with the grace of final perseverance. Now, to this chain of graces there ought to correspond another chain (as it were) of our prayers; if we, by neglecting to pray, break the chain of our prayers, the chain of graces will be broken too; and as it is by this that we have to obtain salvation, we shall not be saved.

It is true that we cannot merit final perseverance, as the Council of Trent teaches: "It cannot be had from any other source but from Him who is able to confirm the man who is standing, that he may stand with perseverance."[100] Nevertheless, says St. Augustine, this great gift of perseverance can in a manner be

---

[100] Sess. 6, c. 13.

merited by our prayers; that is, can be obtained by praying: "This gift, therefore, can be suppliantly merited; that is, can be obtained by supplication."[101] And F. Suarez adds that the man who prays infallibly obtains it. But to obtain it, and to save ourselves, says St. Thomas, a persevering and continual prayer is necessary: "After Baptism continual prayer is necessary to a man in order that he may enter Heaven" (III, q. 39, art. 5). And before this, our Savior Himself had said it over and over again: "We ought always to pray, and not to faint" (Luke 18:1). "Watch ye therefore, praying at all times, that you may be accounted worthy to escape all these things that are to come, and to stand before the Son of man" (Luke 21:36).

The same had been previously said in the Old Testament: "Let nothing hinder thee from praying always" (Eccles. 18:22). "Bless God at all times, and desire Him to direct thy ways" (Job 4:20). Hence the Apostle inculcated on his disciples never to neglect prayer: "Pray without intermission" (1 Thess. 5:17). "Be instant in prayer, watching in it with thanksgiving" (Col. 4:12). "I will therefore that men pray in every place" (1 Tim. 2:8). God does indeed wish to give us perseverance, says St. Nilus, but He will only give it to him who prays for it perseveringly: "He willeth to confer benefits on him who perseveres in prayer."[102] Many sinners, by the help of God's grace, come to be converted and to receive pardon. But then, because they neglect to ask for perseverance, they fall again and lose all.

Nor is it enough, says Bellarmine, to ask the grace of perseverance once or a few times; we ought always to ask it, every day till our death, if we wish to obtain it: "It must be asked day

---

[101] *De Dono pers.* c. 6.
[102] *De Orat.* c. 32.

by day, that it may be obtained day by day." He who asks it one day, obtains it for that one day; but if he does not ask it the next day, the next day he will fall.

And this is the lesson which Our Lord wished to teach us in the parable of the man who would not give his loaves to his friend who asked him for them until he had become importunate in his demand: "Although he will not rise and give because he is his friend, yet because of his importunity, he will rise and give him as many as he needeth" (Luke 11:8). Now if this man, solely to deliver himself from the troublesome importunity of his friend, gave him even against his own will the loaves for which he asked, "how much more," says St. Augustine, "will the good God give, who both commands us to ask, and is angry if we ask not!"[103] How much more will God, who, as He is infinite goodness, has a commensurate desire to communicate to us His good things—how much more will He give His graces when we ask Him for them! And the more, as He Himself tells us to ask for them, and as He is displeased when we do not demand them. God, then, does indeed wish to give us eternal life, and therein all graces; but He wishes also that we should never omit to ask Him for them, even to the extent of being troublesome.

Cornelius à Lapide says on the text just quoted, "God wishes us to be persevering in prayer to the extent of importunity."[104] Men of the world cannot bear the importunate; but God not only bears with them, but wishes us to be importunate in praying to Him for graces, and especially for perseverance. St. Gregory says that God wishes us to do Him violence by our prayers, for such violence does not annoy but pleases Him: "God wills to be

[103] Sermon 61, E. B.
[104] In Luc. xi. 8.

called upon, He wills to be forced, He wills to be conquered by importunity.... Happy violence, by which God is not offended, but appeased!"[105]

So that to obtain perseverance, we must always recommend ourselves to God, morning and night, at meditation, at Mass, at Communion, and always; especially in time of temptation, when we must keep repeating, Lord help me; Lord, assist me; keep Thy hand upon me; leave me not; have pity upon me! Is there anything easier than to say, Lord, help me, assist me! The psalmist says, "With me is prayer to the God of my life" (Ps. 41:9). On which the gloss is as follows: "A man may say, I cannot fast, I cannot give alms; but if he is told to pray, he cannot say this." Because there is nothing easier than to pray. But we must never cease praying; we must (so to speak) continually do violence to God, that He may assist us always — a violence which is delightful and dear to Him. "This violence is grateful to God," says Tertullian;[106] and St. Jerome says that the more persevering and importunate our prayers are, so much the more are they acceptable to God: "Prayer, as long as it is importunate, is more acceptable."[107]

"Blessed is the man that heareth me, and that watcheth daily at my gates" (Prov. 8:34). Happy is that man, says God, who listens to me, and watches continually with holy prayers at the gates of my mercy. And Isaias says, "Blessed are all they that wait for Him" (Isa. 30:18). Blessed are they who, till the end, wait (in prayer) for their salvation from God. Therefore, in the Gospel, Jesus Christ exhorts us to pray. But how? "Ask, and ye shall

[105] *In Ps. paenit* vi.
[106] *Apolog.* c. 39.
[107] *Hom. in Matt.*

receive; seek, and ye shall find; knock, and it shall be opened to you" (Luke 11:9). Would it not have been enough to have said "ask"? Why add "seek" and "knock"? No, it was not superfluous to add them; for thereby our Savior wished us to understand that we ought to do as the poor who go begging. If they do not receive the alms they ask (I speak of licensed beggars), they do not cease asking: they return to ask again; and if the master of the house does not show himself anymore, they set to work to knock at the door, till they become very importunate and troublesome.

That is what God wishes us to do: to pray and to pray again and never leave off praying, that He would assist us and succor us, that He would enlighten us and strengthen us, and never allow us to forfeit His grace. The learned Lessius says that the man cannot be excused from mortal sin who does not pray when he is in sin, or in danger of death; or, again, if he neglects to pray for any notable time, as (he says) for one or two months. But this does not include the time of temptations; because whoever finds himself assailed by any grievous temptation, without doubt sins mortally if he does not have recourse to God in prayer to ask for assistance to resist it; seeing that otherwise he places himself in a proximate, nay, in a certain, occasion of sin.

Why God Delays Granting Us Final Perseverance — Conclusion

But someone will say, since God can give and wishes to give me the grace of perseverance, why does He not give it me all at once, when I ask Him? The holy Fathers assign many reasons:

1. God does not grant it at once but delays it, first, that He may better prove our confidence.

2. And, further, says St. Augustine, that we may long for it more vehemently. Great gifts, he says, should be greatly desired, for good things soon obtained are not

held in the same estimation as those which have been long looked for: "God wills not to give quickly, that you may learn to have great desire for great things; things long desired are pleasanter to obtain, but things 'soon given are cheapened.'"[108]

3. Again, the Lord does so that we may not forget Him; if we were already secure of persevering and of being saved, and if we had not continual need of God's help to preserve us in His grace and to save us, we should soon forget God. Want makes the poor keep resorting to the houses of the rich; so God, to draw us to Himself, as St. Chrysostom says, and to see us often at His feet, in order that He may thus be able to do us greater good, delays giving us the complete grace of salvation till the hour of our death: "It is not because He rejects our prayers that He delays, but by this contrivance He wishes to make us careful, and to draw us to Himself."[109] Again, He does so in order that we, by persevering in prayer, may unite ourselves closer to Him with the sweet bonds of love: "Prayer," says the same St. Chrysostom, "which is accustomed to converse with God, is no slight bond of love to Him."[110] This continual recurrence to God in prayer, and this confident expectation of the graces which we desire from Him, oh, what a great spur and chain is it of love to inflame us and to bind us more closely to God!

---

[108] Sermon 61, E. B.
[109] *In Gen.* hom. 30.
[110] *In Ps.* iv.

Prayer

But till what time have we to pray? Always, says the same saint, till we receive favorable sentence of eternal life; that is to say, till our death: "Do not leave off till you receive."[111] And he goes on to say that the man who resolves, I will never leave off praying till I am saved, will most certainly be saved: "If you say, I will not give in, till I have received, you will assuredly receive." The Apostle writes that many run for the prize, but that he only receives it who runs till he wins: "Know you not that they who run in the race, all run indeed, but one receiveth the prize? So run that you may obtain" (1 Cor. 9:24). It is not, then, enough for salvation simply to pray; but we must pray always, that we may come to receive the crown which God promises, but promises only to those who are constant in prayer till the end.

So that if we wish to be saved, we must do as David did, who always kept his eyes turned to God, to implore His aid against being overcome by his enemies: "My eyes are ever towards the Lord, for He shall pluck my feet out of the snare" (Ps. 24:15). As the devil does not cease continually spreading snares to swallow us up, as St. Peter writes: "Your adversary the devil, as a roaring lion, goeth about, seeking whom he may devour" (1 Peter 5), so ought we ever to stand with our arms in our hands to defend ourselves from such a foe and to say, with the royal prophet, "I will pursue after my enemies; and I will not turn again till they are consumed" (Ps. 17:38). I will never cease fighting till I see my enemies conquered.

But how can we obtain this victory, so important for us, and so difficult? "By most persevering prayers," says St. Augustine—only by prayers, and those most persevering; and till when? As long as the fight shall last. "As the battle is never over," says St.

[111] *In Matt.* hom. 24.

Bonaventure, "so let us never give over asking for mercy."[112] As we must be always in the combat, so should we be always asking God for aid not to be overcome. Woe, says the Wise Man, to him who in this battle leaves off praying: "Woe to them that have lost patience" (Eccles 2:16). We may be saved, the Apostle tells us, but on this condition: "if we retain a firm confidence and the glory of hope until the end" (Heb. 3:6), if we are constant in praying with confidence until death.

Let us, then, take courage from the mercy of God and His promises and say with the same Apostle, "Who then shall separate us from the love of Christ? Shall tribulation, or distress, or danger or persecution, or the sword?" (Rom. 8:35, 37). Who shall succeed in estranging us from the love of Jesus Christ? Tribulation, perhaps, or the danger of losing the goods of this world? The persecutions of devils or men? The torments inflicted by tyrants? "In all these we overcome" (it is St. Paul who encourages us), "because of Him that hath loved us" (Rom. 8:37). No, he says, no tribulation, no misery, danger, persecution, or torture shall ever be able to separate us from the love of Jesus Christ because, with God's help, we shall overcome all, if we fight for love of Him who gave His life for us.

F. Hippolitus Durazzo, the day when he resolved to relinquish his dignity of prelate at Rome and to give himself entirely to God by entering the Society of Jesus (which he afterward did), was so afraid of being faithless by reason of his weakness that he said to God, "Forsake me not, Lord, now that I have given myself wholly to Thee; for pity's sake, do not forsake me!" But he heard the whisper of God in his heart, "Do not thou forsake me; rather," said God, "do I say to thee, Forsake me not." And

---

[112] *De uno Conf.* s. 5.

so at last the servant of God, trusting in His goodness and help, concluded, "Then, O my God, Thou wilt not leave me, and I will not leave Thee."

Finally, if we wish not to be forsaken by God, we ought never to forsake praying to Him not to leave us. If we do thus, He will certainly always assist us and will never allow us to perish and to be separated from His love. And to this end, let us not only take care always to ask for final perseverance, and the graces necessary to obtain it, but let us, at the same time, always by anticipation ask God for grace to go on praying; for this is precisely that great gift which He promised to His elect by the mouth of the prophet: "And I will pour out upon the house of David, and upon the inhabitants of Jerusalem, the spirit of grace and prayers" (Zech. 12:10).

Oh, what a great grace is the spirit of prayer; that is, the grace which God confers on a soul to enable it to pray always! Let us, then, never neglect to beg God to give us this grace and this spirit of continual prayer; because if we pray always, we shall certainly obtain from God perseverance and every other gift which we desire, since His promise of hearing whoever prays to Him cannot fail. "For we are saved by hope" (Rom. 8:24). With this hope of always praying, we may reckon ourselves saved. "Confidence will give us a broad entrance into this city."[113] This hope, said Venerable Bede, will give us a safe passage into the city of Paradise.

[113] *In solemn. omn. SS. hom. 2.*

Part II

The Grace of Prayer Given to All and This Grace's Ordinary Mode of Operation

Introduction

Taking, then, for granted that prayer is necessary for the attainment of eternal life, as we have proved in part I, chapter I, we should consequently also take for granted that everyone has sufficient aid from God to enable him actually to pray, without need of any further special grace; and that by prayer he may obtain all other graces necessary to enable him to persevere in keeping the Commandments and so gain eternal life; so that no one who is lost can ever excuse himself by saying that it was through want of the aid necessary for his salvation. For as God, in the natural order, has ordained that man should be born naked and in want of several things necessary for life but then has given him hands and intelligence to clothe himself and provide for his other needs, so, in the supernatural order, man is born unable to obtain salvation by his own strength; but God in His goodness grants to everyone the grace of prayer, by which he is able to obtain all other graces which he needs in order to keep the Commandments and to be saved.

But before I explain this point, I must prove two preliminary propositions. First, that God wills all men to be saved and, therefore, that Jesus Christ has died for all. Secondly, that God, on His part, gives to all men the graces necessary for salvation whereby everyone may be saved if he corresponds to them.

Chapter 1

God Wishes All Men to Be Saved, and Therefore Christ Died to Save All Men

1. God Wishes All Men to Be Saved

God loves all things that He has created: "For Thou lovest all things that are, and hatest none of the things that Thou hast made" (Wisd. 11:25). Now love cannot be idle: "All love has a force of its own, and cannot be idle," says St. Augustine. Hence love necessarily implies benevolence, so that the person who loves cannot help doing good to the person beloved whenever there is an opportunity: "Love persuades a man to do those things which he believes to be good for him whom he loves," says Aristotle.[114] If, then, God loves all men, He must in consequence will that all should obtain eternal salvation, which is the one and sovereign good of man, seeing that it is the one end for which he was created: "You have your fruit unto sanctification; and the end life everlasting" (Rom. 6:22).

This doctrine, that God wishes all men to be saved and that Jesus Christ died for the salvation of all, is now a certain doctrine taught by the Catholic Church, as theologians in common teach, namely, Petavius, Gonet, Gotti, and others, besides Tourneley, who adds that it is a doctrine all but of faith.

---

[114] *Rhetor.* 1. 2, c. 4.

Prayer

Decision of the Church

With reason, therefore, were the predestinarians condemned, who, among their errors, taught that God does not will all men to be saved; as Hincmar, archbishop of Rheims, testifies of them in his first letter, where he says, "The ancient predestinarians asserted that God does not will all men to be saved, but only those who are saved." These persons were condemned, first in the Council of Arles, A.D. 475, which pronounced "anathema to him that said that Christ did not die for all men, and that He does not will all to be saved."[115] They were next condemned in the Council of Lyons, A.D. 490, where Lucidus was forced to retract and confess, "I condemn the man who says that Christ did not suffer death for the salvation of all men." So also in the ninth century, Gotheschalcus, who renewed the same error, was condemned by the Council of Quercy, A.D. 853, in the third article of which it was decided, "God wills all men, without exception, to be saved, although all men be not saved"; and in the fourth article: "There is no man for whom Christ did not suffer, although all men be not redeemed by the mystery of His Passion."[116] The same error was finally condemned in the 12th and 13th Propositions of Quesnel. In the former, it was said: "When God wills to save a soul, the will of God is undoubtedly effectual"; in the latter: "All whom God wills to save through Christ are infallibly saved." These propositions were justly condemned, precisely because they meant that God does not will all men to be saved; since from the proposition that those whom God wills to be saved are infallibly saved, it logically follows that God does not will even all the faithful to be saved, let alone all men.

[115] *Anathema* 6.
[116] Article 3, 4.

This was also clearly expressed by the Council of Trent, in which it was said that Jesus Christ died "that all might receive the adoption of sons", and in chapter 3: "but though He died for all, yet all do not receive the benefits of His death."[117] The Council then takes for granted that the Redeemer died not only for the elect but also for those who, through their own fault, do not receive the benefit of Redemption. Nor is it of any use to affirm that the Council only meant to say that Jesus Christ has given to the world a ransom sufficient to save all men; for in this sense, we might say that He died also for the devils. Moreover, the Council of Trent intended here to reprove the errors of those innovators who, not denying that the blood of Christ was sufficient to save all, yet asserted that in fact it was not shed and given for all; that is the error which the Council intended to condemn when it said that Our Savior died for all.

Further, in chapter 6, it says that sinners are put in a fit state to receive justification by hope in God through the merits of Jesus Christ: "They are raised to hope, trusting that God will be merciful to them through Christ."[118] Now, if Jesus Christ had not applied to all the merits of His Passion, then, since no one (without a special revelation) could be certain of being among the number of those to whom the Redeemer had willed to apply the fruit of His merits, no sinner could entertain such hope, not having the certain and secure foundation which is necessary for hope; namely, that God wills all men to be saved and will pardon all sinners prepared for it by the merits of Jesus Christ. And this, besides being the error formerly condemned in Baius, who said that Christ had only died for the elect, is also condemned in

---

[117] Session 6, c. 2–3.
[118] Session 6, c. 6.

the fifth proposition of Jansenius: "It is Semi-Pelagianism to say that Christ died or shed His Blood for all men." And Innocent X, in his Constitution of A.D. 1653, expressly declared that to say Christ died for the salvation of the elect only is an impious and heretical proposition.

The Celebrated Text of St. Paul

On the other hand, both the Scriptures and all the Fathers assure us that God sincerely and really wishes the salvation of all men and the conversion of all sinners, as long as they are in this world. For this we have, first of all, the express text of St. Paul: "Who will have all men to be saved, and to come to the knowledge of the truth." The sentence of the apostle is absolute and indicative "Who will have all men to be saved, and to come to the knowledge of the truth" (1 Tim. 2:4). These words in their natural sense declare that God truly wills all men to be saved; and it is a certain rule, received in common by all, that the words in Scripture are not to be distorted to an unnatural sense, except in the sole case when the literal meaning is repugnant to faith or morals. St. Bonaventure writes precisely to our purpose when he says, "We must hold that when the apostle says, God wills all men to be saved, it is necessary to grant that He does will it."[119]

It is true that St. Augustine and St. Thomas mention different interpretations which have been given to this text; but both these Doctors understand it to mean a real will of God to save all, without exception.

And concerning St. Augustine, we shall see just now that this was his true opinion; so that St. Prosper protests against attributing to him the supposition that God did not sincerely wish the

---

[119] *In 1 Sent.* d. 46, a. I, q. I.

salvation of all men, and of each individual, as an aspersion on the holy Doctor. Hence the same St. Prosper, who was a most faithful disciple of his, says, "It is most sincerely to be believed and confessed that God wills all men to be saved; since the apostle (whose very words these are) is particular in commanding that prayers should be made to God for all."[120]

The argument of the saint is clear, founded on St. Paul's words in the above-cited passage: "I beseech therefore, first of all that prayers should be made for all men," and then he adds, "For, this is good and acceptable before God our Savior, who wills all men to be saved." So the apostle wishes us to pray for all, exactly in the same sense that God wishes the salvation of all. St. Chrysostom uses the same argument: "If He wills all to be saved, surely we ought to pray for all. If He desires all to be saved, do you also be of one mind with Him."[121] And if in some passages in his controversy with the Semi-Pelagians, St. Augustine seems to have held a different interpretation of this text, saying that God does not will the salvation of each individual, but only of some, Petavius well observes that here the holy Father speaks only incidentally, not with direct intention; or, at any rate, that he speaks of the grace of that absolute and victorious will (*voluntas absoluta et victrix*) with which God absolutely wills the salvation of some persons, and of which the saint elsewhere says, "The will of the Almighty is always invincible."[122]

Let us hear how St. Thomas uses another method of reconciling the opinion of St. Augustine with that of St. John Damascene, who holds that antecedently God wills all and each individual

---

[120] Resp. ad 2 obj. Vincent.
[121] *In I Tim.* hom. 7.
[122] *Enchir.* c. 102.

to be saved: "God's first intention is to will all men to be saved, that as good He may make us partakers of His goodness; but after we have sinned, He wills to punish us as just."[123] On the other hand, St. Augustine (as we have seen) seems in a few passages to think differently. But St. Thomas reconciles these opinions and says that St. Damascene spoke of the antecedent will of God, by which He really wills all men to be saved, while St. Augustine spoke of the consequent will. He then goes on to explain the meaning of antecedent and consequent will: "Antecedent will is that by which God wills all to be saved; but when all the circumstances of this or that individual are considered, it is found to be good that all men should be saved; for it is good that he who prepares himself, and consents to it, should be saved; but not he who is unwilling and resists, etc. And this is called the consequent will, because it presupposes a foreknowledge of a man's deeds, not as a cause of the act of will, but as a reason for the thing willed and determined."

So that St. Thomas was also of the opinion that God truly wills all men and each individual to be saved. This opinion he reasserts in several other places. On the text "Him that cometh to me, I will not cast out" (John 6:37), he quotes St. Chrysostom, who makes Our Lord say, "If then I was incarnate for the salvation of men, how can I cast them out?" And this is what He means when He says, "Therefore I cast them not out, because I came down from Heaven to do my Father's will, who wills all men to be saved."[124] And again, "God, by His most liberal will, gives (grace) to everyone that prepares himself," who wills all men to be saved; "and therefore the grace of God is wanting to no man, but as far

[123] *De Fid. orth.* 1. 2, c. 29.
[124] *In Joan.* vi. lect. 4.

as He is concerned, He communicates it to everyone."[125] Again, he declares the same thing more expressly in his explanation of the text of St. Paul "God wills all men to be saved." "In God," he says, "the salvation of all men, considered in itself, belongs to that class of things which He wishes, and this is His antecedent will; but when the good of justice is taken into consideration, and the rightness of punishing sin, in this sense He does not will the salvation of all, and this is His consequent will."[126] Here we may see how consistent St. Thomas was in his explanation of antecedent and consequent will; for he here repeats what he had said in the passage quoted a little before. In this place he only adds the comparison of a merchant, who antecedently wills to save all his merchandise; but if a tempest comes on, he willingly throws it overboard, in order to preserve his own life. In like manner, he says, God, considering the iniquity of some persons, wills them to be punished in satisfaction of His justice, and consequently does not will them to be saved; but antecedently, and considered in itself, He wills with a true desire the salvation of all men. So that, as he says in the former passage, God's will to save all men is on His part absolute; it is only conditional on the part of the object willed, that is, if man will correspond to what the right order demands, in order to be saved. "Nor yet," he says, "is there imperfection on the part of God's will, but on the part of the thing willed; because it is not accepted with all the circumstances which are required, in order to be saved in the proper manner."[127] And he again and more distinctly declares what he means by antecedent and consequent will: "A judge antecedently wishes

---

[125] *In Heb.* xii. lect. 3
[126] *In 1 Tim. ii.* Lect. I.
[127] *In 1 Sent.* d. 46, q. 1, a. 1.

every man to live, but he consequently wishes a murderer to be hanged; so God antecedently wills every man to be saved, but He consequently wills some to be damned; in consequence, that is, of the exigencies of His justice" (I, q. 19, art. 6).

It is certain that God creates all men for eternal life. We ought to submit ourselves to the will of God, who has chosen to leave this mystery in obscurity to His Church, that we all might humble ourselves under the deep judgments of His Divine Providence, and the more, because divine grace, by which alone men can gain eternal life, is dispensed more or less abundantly by God entirely gratuitously, and without any regard to our merits. So that to save ourselves it will always be necessary for us to throw ourselves into the arms of the divine mercy, in order that He may assist us with His grace to obtain salvation, trusting always in His infallible promises to hear and save the man who prays to Him.

Other Texts of Scripture

But let us return to our point, that God sincerely wills all men to be saved. There are other texts which prove the same thing, as when God says: "As I live, saith the Lord, I desire not the death of the wicked, but that the wicked man turn from his way and live (Ezek. 33:11). He not only says that He wills not the death, but that He wills the life of a sinner; and He swears, as Tertullian observes, in order that He may be more readily believed in this: "When moreover He swears, saying, as I live, He desires to be believed."[128]

Further, David says: "For wrath is in His indignation, and life in His good will" (Ps. 29:6). If He chastises us, He does it because our sins provoke Him to indignation; but as to His will, He wills

---

[128] *De Paenit.*

not our death, but our life: "Life is His will." St. Basil says about this text that God wills all to be made partakers of life. David says elsewhere: "Our God is the God of salvation; and of the Lord, of the Lord are the issues from death" (Ps. 67:21). On this Bellarmine says: "This is proper to Him, this is His nature, our God is a saving God, and His are the issues from death—that is, liberation from it"; so that it is God's proper nature to save all and to deliver all from eternal death.

Again, Our Lord says: "Come to me, all ye that labor and are burdened, and I will refresh you" (Matt. 11:28). If He calls all to salvation, then He truly wills all to be saved. Again, St. Peter says: "The Lord dealeth patiently for your sake, not willing that any should perish, but that all should return to penance" (2 Pet. 3:9). He does not will the damnation of anyone, but He wills that all should do penance and so should be saved.

Again, Our Lord says: "I stand at the gate and knock. If any man shall hear my voice, and open to me the door, I will come in to him" (Rev. 3:20). "Why will you die, O house of Israel? Return and live" (Ezek. 18:31–32). "What is there that I ought to do more to my vineyard, that I have not done to it?" (Isa. 5:4). "How often would I have gathered together thy children, as the hen gathereth her chickens under her wings, and thou wouldest not!" (Matt. 23:37). How could Our Lord have said that He stands knocking at the heart of us sinners? How exhort us so strongly to return to His arms? How reproach us by asking what more He could have done for our salvation? How say that He has willed to receive us as children, if He had not a true will to save all men? Again, St. Luke relates that Our Lord, looking over Jerusalem from a distance, and contemplating the destruction of its people because of their sin: "Seeing the city, He wept over it" (Luke 19:41). Why did He weep then, says Theophylact (after St. Chrysostom), seeing the ruin of the Jews, unless it was because He really desired their salvation? Now then, after so many attestations of Our Lord, in which He makes known to us that He wills to see all men saved, how can it ever be said that God does not will the salvation of all? "But if these texts of Scripture," says Petavius, "in which God has testified His will in such clear and often-repeated expressions, nay even with tears and with an oath, may be abused and distorted to the very opposite sense—namely, that God determined to send all mankind (except a few) to perdition, and never had a will to save them, what dogma of faith is so clear as to be safe from similar injury and cavil?"[129] This great writer says that to deny that God really wills the salvation of all men is an insult and cavil against the plainest doctrines of the Faith. And Cardinal Sfondrati adds: "Those who think otherwise seem to me to make God a mere stage-god; like those people who pretend to be kings in a play, when indeed they are anything but kings."[130]

General Consent of the Fathers

Moreover, this truth, that God wills all men to be saved, is confirmed by the general consent of the Fathers. There can be no doubt that all the Greek Fathers have been uniform in saying that God wills all and each individual to be saved. So St. Justin, St. Basil, St. Gregory, St. Cyril, St. Methodius, and St. Chrysostom, all adduced by Petavius. But let us see what the Latin Fathers say:

> St. Jerome: (God) "wills to save all; but since no man is saved without his own will, He wills us to will what

[129] *De Deo. lib.* 10, c. 15, n. 5.
[130] Nodus praed. p. I, § I.

is good, that when we have willed, He may also will to fulfill His designs in us";[131] and in another place, "God therefore willed to save those who desire (to be saved); and He invited them to salvation, that their will might have its reward; but they would not believe in Him."[132]

St. Hilary: "God would that all men were saved, and not those alone who are to belong to the number of the elect, but all absolutely, so as to make no exception."[133]

St. Paulinus: "Christ says to all, 'Come to me,' etc.; for He, the Creator of all men, so far as He is concerned, wills every man to be saved."[134]

St. Ambrose: "Even with respect to the wicked He had to manifest His will (to save them), and therefore He could not pass over His betrayer, that all might see that in the election even of the traitor He exhibits (His desire) of saving all ... and, so far as God is concerned, He shows to all that He was willing to deliver all."[135]

The author of the work known as the *Commentaries of St. Ambrose* (supposed by Petavius to be Hilary the Second) in speaking of the text of St. Paul, "Who wills all men," etc., asks this question: "But since God wills that all should be saved, as He is Almighty, why are there so many who are not saved?" And he answers: "He wills them to be saved, if they also are willing; for

---

[131] *In Eph.* i.
[132] *In Is.* lxiii.
[133] *Ep. ad Aug.*
[134] *Ep.* 24. *ad Sever.*
[135] *De Parad.* c. 8.

He who gave the law excluded no one from salvation … this medicine is of no use to the unwilling." He says that God has excluded no one from glory and that He gives grace to all to be saved, but on condition that they are willing to correspond to it because His grace is of no use to the man who rejects it. St. Chrysostom, in like manner, asks, "Why then are not all men saved, if God wills all to be saved?" And he answers, "Because every man's will does not coincide with His will, and He forces no man."[136] St. Augustine: "God wills all men to be saved, but not so as to destroy their free will."[137]

2. Jesus Christ Died to Save All Men

That Jesus Christ, therefore, died for all and each of mankind, is clear, not only from the Scriptures but from the writings of the Fathers. Great, certainly, was the ruin which the sin of Adam occasioned to the whole human race; but Jesus Christ, by the grace of Redemption, repaired all the evils which Adam introduced. Hence the Council of Trent has declared that Baptism renders the soul pure and immaculate and that the sin which remains in it is not for its harm, but to enable it to gain a higher crown, if it resists so as not to consent to it: "For in the regenerate God hates nothing … they are made innocent, immaculate, pure, and beloved of God.… But this holy synod confesses and feels that concupiscence or the fuel (of sin) remains in Baptized persons; but as it was left for our probation, it cannot injure those who do not consent to it; nay rather, he who contends lawfully (against it) shall be crowned."[138] Thus, as Saint Leo says, "we have gained

---

[136] *De Mut. nom. hom.* 3, E. B.
[137] *De Spir. et Litt.* c. 33.
[138] Sess. 5, De pecc. or. n. 5.

greater things by the grace of Christ than we had lost through the envy of the devil."[139]

The gain which we have made by the redemption of Jesus Christ is greater than the loss which we suffered by the sin of Adam. The Apostle plainly declared this when he said, "Not as the offense, so also the gift. And where sin abounded, grace did more abound" (Rom. 5:15, 20). Our Lord says the same: "I am come that they may have life, and have it more abundantly" (John 10:10). David and Isaiah had predicted it: "With Him is plentiful redemption. — She hath received of the hand of the Lord double for all her sins" (Ps. 129:7; Isa. 40:2). About which words the interpreter says: "God has so forgiven iniquities through Christ, that men have received double — that is, very much greater good, instead of the punishment of sin which they deserved."

Now that our Savior, as I said, died for all, and that He offered the work of His redemption to the Eternal Father for the salvation of each one, the Holy Scriptures assures us of the following.

The Testimony of Holy Scripture

"The Son of Man is come to save that which was lost" (Matt. 18:11). "Who gave Himself a redemption for all" (1 Tim. 2:6). "And Christ died for all; that they also who live, may not now live to themselves, but to Him who died for them" (2 Cor. 5:15). "For therefore we labor and are reviled, because we hope in the living God, who is the Savior of all men, especially of the faithful" (1 Tim. 4:10). "And He is the propitiation for our sins; and not for ours only, but also for those of the whole world" (1 John 2:2). "For the charity of Christ presseth us, judging this that, if one died for all, then all were dead" (2 Cor. 5:14). And to speak

---

[139] *De Asc.* s. i.

only of this last text, I ask, how could the Apostle ever have concluded that all were dead, because Christ died for all, unless he had been certain that Christ had really died for all?

And the more, because St. Paul uses this truth as an argument for the love which it should kindle in us toward Our Savior. But by far the best passage to exhibit the desire and wish which God has to save all men is another text of St. Paul: "He that spared not even His own Son, but delivered Him up for us all" (Rom. 8:32). The force of this passage is increased by what follows: "How hath He not also, with Him, given us all things" (Rom. 8:32). If God has given us all things, how can we henceforth fear that He has denied us the election to glory, always on condition that we correspond (to His grace)? And if He has given us His Son, says Cardinal Sfondrati, how will He deny us the grace to be saved? "Here he clearly instructs us [he is speaking of St. Paul] that God assures us that He will not refuse us the less after He has given the greater; that He will not deny us grace to save ourselves, after giving His Son that we might be saved."[140] And in truth, how could St. Paul have said that God, in giving us His Son, has given us all things, if the Apostle had believed that God had excluded many from the glory which is the one good and the one end for which they were created? Has then God given "all things" to these "many" and yet denied them the best thing—namely, eternal happiness, without which (as there is no middle way) they cannot but be eternally miserable? Unless we would say another thing still more unseemly, as another learned author well observes—namely, that God gives to all the grace to attain glory, but then refuses to allow many to enter on its enjoyment; that He gives the means, and refuses the end.

[140] Nod. Praed. p. I, § 2. n. II.

The Teaching of the Holy Fathers

For the rest, all the holy Fathers agree in saying that Jesus Christ died to obtain eternal salvation for all men.

St. Jerome: "Christ died for all; He was the only One who could be offered for all, because all were dead in sins."[141]

St. Ambrose: "Christ came to cure our wounds; but since all do not search for the remedy, therefore He cures those who are willing; He does not force the unwilling."[142] In another place: "He has provided for all men the means of cure, that whoever perishes may lay the blame of his death on himself, because he would not be cured when he had a remedy; and that, on the other hand, the mercy of Christ to all may be openly proclaimed, who wills that all men should be saved."[143] And more clearly still in another place: "Jesus did not write His will for the benefit of one, or of few, but of all; we are all inscribed therein as His heirs; the legacy is in common, and belongs by right to all; the universal heritage, belonging wholly to each."[144] Mark the words "We are all inscribed as heirs of Heaven."

St. Leo: "As Christ found no one free from guilt, so He came to deliver all."[145]

St. Augustine, on the words of St. John, "For God did not send His Son to judge the world, but that the world might

---

[141] *In 2 Cor.* v.
[142] *In Ps.* lxxii.
[143] *De Abel.* l. 2 c. 3.
[144] *In Ps.* cxviii. s. 14.
[145] *In Nat. Dom.* s. I

be saved through Him," says: "So, as far as it lies with the Physician, He came to heal the sick man."[146] Mark the words "as far as it lies with the Physician." For God, as far as He is concerned, effectually wills the salvation of all, but (as St. Augustine goes on to say) cannot heal the man who will not be healed: "He heals universally, but He heals not the unwilling.[147] For what can be happier for thee than, as thou hast thy life in thy hands, so to have thy health depend on thy will?" When he says "He heals," he speaks of sinners who are sick and unable to get well by their own strength; when he says "universally" (*omnino*), he declares that nothing is wanting on God's part for sinners to be healed and saved. Then, when he says "as thou hast thy life in thy hands, so thy health depends on thy will," he shows that God, for His part, really wills us all to be saved; otherwise, it would not be in our power to obtain health and eternal life. In another place, "He who redeemed us at such a cost wills not that we perish; for He does not purchase in order to destroy, but He redeems in order to give life."[148] He has redeemed us all, in order to save us all. And hence he encourages all to hope for eternal bliss in that celebrated sentence: "Let human frailty raise itself; let it not say, I shall never be happy.... It is a greater thing that Christ has done than that which He has promised. What has He done? He has died for thee. What has He promised? That thou shalt live with Him."[149]

---

[146] *In Jo. tr.* 12.
[147] *In Ps.* cii.
[148] Sermon 22, E. B.
[149] *In Ps.* cxlviii.

Some have pretended to say that Jesus Christ offered His Blood for all in order to obtain grace for them, but not salvation. But Petrocorensis will not hear of this opinion, of which he says: "O disputatious frivolity! How could the wisdom of God will the means of salvation without willing its end?"[150] St. Augustine, moreover, speaking against the Jews, says: "Ye acknowledge the side which ye pierced, that it was opened both by you and for you."[151] If Jesus Christ had not really given His Blood for all, the Jews might have answered St. Augustine that it was quite true they had opened the side of our Savior but not that it was opened for them.

In like manner, St. Thomas has no doubt that Jesus Christ died for all; whence he deduces that He wills all to be saved: "Christ Jesus is mediator between God and men; not between God and some men, but between Him and all men; and this would not be, unless He willed all to be saved."[152] This is confirmed, as we have already said, by the condemnation of the fifth proposition of Jansenius, who said, "It is semi-Pelagianism to assert that Christ died or shed His Blood for all men." The sense of this, according to the context of the other condemned propositions, and according to the principles of Jansenius, is as follows: Jesus Christ did not die to merit for all men the graces sufficient for salvation, but only for the predestined; or, in Jansenius's own expressed words, "It is in no way consonant to the principles of Augustine, to think that Christ Our Lord died or shed His Blood for the eternal salvation either of unbelievers who die in their unbelief or of the just who do not

---

[150] *Lib*. iii. c. 3, q. 4.
[151] *De Symb. ad cat*. 1. 2, c. 8.
[152] *In I Tim*. ii. led. I.

persevere."[153] Therefore the contrary and Catholic belief is as follows: It is not Semi-Pelagianism, but it is right to say that Jesus Christ died to merit not only for the predestinate but for all, even for the reprobate, grace sufficient to obtain eternal salvation in the ordinary course of Providence.

Further, that God truly, on His part, wills all men to be saved, and that Jesus Christ died for the salvation of all, is certified to us by the fact that God imposes on us all the precept of hope. The reason is clear. St. Paul calls Christian hope the anchor of the soul, secure and firm: "Who have fled for refuge to hold fast the hope set before us. Which we have as an anchor of the soul, sure and firm" (Heb. 6:18, 19). Now in what could we fix this sure and firm anchor of our hope except in the truth that God wills all to be saved? "With what confidence," says Petrocorensis, "will men be able to hope for God's mercy if it is not certain that God wills the salvation of all of them? With what confidence will they offer the death of Christ to God, in order to obtain pardon, if it is uncertain whether He was offered up for them?"[154] And Cardinal Sfondrati says that if God had elected some to eternal life and excluded others, we should have a greater motive to despair than to hope, seeing that, in fact, the elect are much fewer than the damned: "No one could have a firm hope, since he would have more grounds of despair than of hope; for the reprobate are much more numerous than the elect."[155] And if Jesus Christ had not died for the salvation of all, how could we have a sure ground to hope for salvation through the merits of Jesus Christ without a special revelation? But St. Augustine

[153] *De Grat. Chr.* c. 20.
[154] *Lib.* 3, c. 3, q. 4.
[155] *Nod. praed.* p. I. § I.

had no doubt when he said, "All my hope, and the certainty of my faith, is in the Precious Blood of Christ, which was shed for us and for our salvation."[156] Thus the saint placed all his hope in the Blood of Jesus Christ; because the faith assured him that Christ died for all.

3. Children Who Die without Baptism

Here it only remains for us to answer the objection which is drawn from children being lost when they die before Baptism, and before they come to the use of reason. If God wills all to be saved, it is objected, how is it that these children perish without any fault of their own, since God gives them no assistance to attain eternal salvation? There are two answers to this objection, the latter more correct than the former. I will state them briefly.

First, it is answered that God, by antecedent will, wishes all to be saved and therefore has granted universal means for the salvation of all; but these means at times fail of their effect, either by reason of the unwillingness of some persons to avail themselves of them or because others are unable to make use of them, on account of secondary causes (such as the death of children), whose course God is not bound to change, after having disposed the whole according to the just judgment of His general Providence; all this is collected from what St. Thomas says: Jesus Christ offered His merits for all men and instituted Baptism for all; but the application of this means of salvation, so far as relates to children who die before the use of reason, is not prevented by the direct will of God, but by a merely permissive will; because as He is the general provider of all things,

---

[156] *Medit.* c. 14.

He is not bound to disturb the general order, to provide for the particular order.

The second answer is that to perish is not the same as not to be blessed since eternal happiness is a gift entirely gratuitous, and therefore the want of it is not a punishment. The opinion, therefore, of St. Thomas is very just: that children who die in infancy have neither the pain of sense nor the pain of loss; not the pain of sense, he says, "because pain of sense corresponds to conversion to creatures; and in Original Sin there is not conversion to creatures" (as the fault is not our own), "and therefore pain of sense is not due to Original Sin" because Original Sin does not imply an act.[157] Objectors oppose to this the teaching of St. Augustine, who in some places shows that his opinion was that children are condemned even to the pain of sense. But in another place he declares that he was very much confused about this point. These are his words: "When I come to the punishment of infants, I find myself (believe me) in great straits; nor can I at all find anything to say."[158] And in another place he writes that it may be said that such children receive neither reward nor punishment: "Nor need we fear that it is impossible there should be a middle sentence between reward and punishment; since their life was midway between sin and good works."[159] This was directly affirmed by St. Gregory Nazianzen: "Children will be sentenced by the just judge neither to the glory of Heaven nor to punishment."[160] St. Gregory of Nyssa was of the same opinion: "The premature

---

[157] *De Mal.* q. 5, a. 2.
[158] Epistle 166 E. B.
[159] *De Lib.* Ar. 1, 3, c. 23.
[160] *Serm. in S. Lav.*

death of children shows that they who have thus ceased to live will not be in pain and unhappiness."[161]

And as far as relates to the pain of loss, although these children are excluded from glory, nevertheless St. Thomas,[162] who had reflected most deeply on this point, teaches that no one feels pain for the want of that good of which he is not capable; so that, as no man grieves that he cannot fly, or no private person that he is not emperor, so these children feel no pain at being deprived of the glory of which they were never capable; since they could never pretend to it either by the principles of nature or by their own merits. St. Thomas adds, in another place,[163] a further reason, which is that the supernatural knowledge of glory comes only by means of actual faith, which transcends all natural knowledge; so that children can never feel pain for the privation of that glory, of which they never had a supernatural knowledge. He further says, in the former passage, that such children will not only not grieve for the loss of eternal happiness but will, moreover, have pleasure in their natural gifts and will even in some way enjoy God, so far as is implied in natural knowledge and in natural love: "Rather will they rejoice in this, that they will participate much in the divine goodness and in natural perfections." And he immediately adds, that although they will be separated from God, as regards the union of glory, nevertheless "they will be united with Him by participation of natural gifts; and so will even be able to rejoice in Him with a natural knowledge and love."[164]

---

[161] *De Infant*, etc.
[162] *In 2 Sent*. d. 33, q. 2, a. 2.
[163] *De Mal*. q. 5, a. 3.
[164] *In 2 Sent*. d. 33, q. 2, a. 2.

Chapter 2

·••⧯•••⧯••·

God Gives to All the Just the Grace Necessary for Observance of the Commandments, and to All Sinners the Grace Necessary for Conversion

1. Proofs

If, then, God wills all to be saved, it follows that He gives to all that grace and those aids which are necessary for the attainment of salvation; otherwise it could never be said that He has a true will to save all. "The effect of the antecedent will," says St. Thomas, "by which God wills the salvation of all men, is that order of nature the purpose of which is our salvation, and likewise those things which conduce to that end, and which are offered to all in common, whether by nature or by grace."[165] It is certain, in contradiction to the blasphemies of Luther and Calvin, that God does not impose a law that is impossible to be observed. On the other hand, it is certain, that without the assistance of grace, the observance of the law is impossible; as Innocent I declared against the Pelagians when he said, "It is

---

[165] *In 1 Sent.* d. 46. q. I. a. I.

certain, that as we overcome by the aid of God, so without His aid we must be overcome."[166] Pope Celestine declared the same thing. Therefore, if God gives to all men a possible law, it follows that He also gives to all men the grace necessary to observe it, whether immediately or mediately, by means of prayer, as the Council of Trent has most clearly defined: "God does not command impossibilities; but by commanding He admonishes you both to do what you can, and to ask for that which is beyond your power, and by His help enables you to do it."[167] Otherwise, if God refused us both the proximate and remote grace to enable us to fulfill the law, either the law would have been given in vain, or sin would be necessary, and if necessary, would be no longer sin, as we shall shortly prove at some length.

Teaching of the Fathers of the Greek Church

And this is the general opinion of the Greek Fathers:

St. Cyril of Alexandria says: "But if a man endowed as others, and equally with them, with the gifts of divine grace, has fallen by his own free will, how shall Christ be said not to have saved even him, since He delivered the man and gave him the necessary aid to avoid sin?"[168] How, says the saint, can that sinner, who has received the assistance of grace equally with those who remained faithful and has of his own accord chosen to sin, how can he blame Jesus Christ, who has, as far as He is concerned, delivered him by means of the assistance granted to him? St. John Chrysostom asks: "How is it that some are vessels of wrath,

---

[166] *Rescr. ad Conc. Carthag.*
[167] Session 6, Cap. 11.
[168] In Jo, l. II. c. 21.

others vessels of mercy?" And he answers, "Because of each person's free will; for, since God is very good, He manifests equal kindness to all." Then, speaking of Pharaoh, whose heart is said in Scripture to have been hardened, he adds, "If Pharaoh was not saved, it must all be attributed to his will, since no less was given to him than to those who were saved."[169] And in another place, speaking of the petition of the mother of Zebedee's sons, on the words "It is not mine to give," etc. (Matt. 20:23), he observes: "By this Christ wished to show that it was not simply His to give, but that it also belonged to the combatants to take; for if it depended only on Himself, all men would be saved."[170]

St. Isidore of Pelusium: "For God wills seriously, and in all ways, to assist those who are wallowing in vice, that He may deprive them of all excuse."[171]

St. Cyril of Jerusalem: "God has opened the gate of eternal life, so that, as far as He is concerned, all may gain it without anything to hinder them."[172]

But the doctrine of these Greek Fathers does not suit Jansenius, who has the temerity to say that they have spoken most imperfectly on grace: "None have spoken in grace more imperfectly than the Greeks." In matters of grace, then, are we not to follow the teaching of the Greek Fathers, who were the first masters and columns of the Church? Perhaps the doctrine of the Greeks, especially in this important matter, was different from that of the

[169] *In Rom.* hom. 16.
[170] *Hom, in loco cit. cont. Anom.*
[171] *Lib.* 2. cp. 270.
[172] *Catech.* 18.

Latin Church? On the contrary, it is certain that the true doctrine of faith came from the Greek to the Latin Church; so that, as St. Augustine wrote against Julian, who opposed to him the authority of the Greek Fathers, there can be no doubt that the faith of the Latins is the same as that of the Greeks. Whom, then, are we to follow? Shall we follow Jansenius, whose errors have already been condemned as heretical by the Church; who had the audacity to say that even the just have not the grace requisite to enable them to keep certain precepts; and that man merits and demerits, even though he acts through necessity, provided he is not forced by violence; these are all his other errors springing from his most false system of "the delectation relatively victorious."

Teaching of the Fathers of the Latin Church

But since the Greek Fathers do not satisfy Jansenius, let us see what the Latins say on this subject. But they in no wise differ from the Greeks.

> St. Jerome says, "Man can do no good work without God, who, in giving free will, did not refuse His grace to aid every single work."[173] Mark the words "did not refuse His grace for every single work."

> St. Ambrose: "He would never come and knock at the door, unless He wished to enter; it is our fault that He does not always enter."[174]

> St. Leo: "Justly does He insist on the command; since He furnishes beforehand aid to keep it."[175]

---

[173] *Ep. ad Cyprian, presb.*
[174] *In Ps.* cxviii. s. 12.
[175] *De Pass.* s. 16.

St. Hilary: "Now the grace of justification has abounded through one gift to all men."[176]

Innocent I: "He gives to man daily remedies; and unless we put confidence in them and depend upon them, we shall never be able to overcome human errors."[177]

St. Augustine: "It is not imputed to you as a sin if you are ignorant against your will, but if you neglect to learn that of which you are ignorant. Nor is it imputed as a sin that you do not bind up your wounded limbs, but (mark these words) that you despise Him who is willing to cure you. These are your own sins; for no man is deprived of the knowledge of how to seek with benefit to himself." In another place: "Therefore if the soul is ignorant of what it is to do, it proceeds from this, that it has not yet learned; but it will receive this knowledge if it has made a good use of what it has already received; for it has received in this that it can piously and diligently seek, if it will"; (mark the words) "it has received power to seek piously and diligently."[178]

So that everyone receives at least the remote grace to seek; and if he makes good use of this, he will receive the proximate grace to perform that which at first he could not do. St. Augustine founds all this on the principle that no man sins in doing that which he cannot help; therefore, if a man sins in anything, he sins in that he might have avoided it by the grace of God, which is wanting to no man: "Who sins in that which cannot in any

[176] *In Ps.* lix.
[177] *Rescr. ad Conc. Carthag.*
[178] *De Lib. Arb.* 1. 3, c. 19, 22.

way be helped? But a man does sin; therefore it might have been helped."[179] "But only by His aid, who cannot be deceived."[180] An evident reason, by which it becomes quite clear … (that when we speak of the sin of the obstinate) that if the grace necessary to observe the Commandments were wanting, there would be no sin.

St. Thomas teaches the same in several places. In one place, in explaining the text "who will have all men to be saved" (1 Tim. 2:4), he says, "and therefore grace is wanting to no man, but (as far as God is concerned) is communicated to all; as the sun is present even to the blind."[181] So that as the sun sheds its light upon all, and only those are deprived of it who voluntarily blind themselves to its rays, so God communicates to all men grace to observe the law; and men are lost simply because they will not avail themselves of it. In another place: "It belongs to Divine Providence to provide all men with what is necessary to salvation, if only there be no impediment on man's part."[182] If, then, God gives all men the graces necessary for salvation, and if actual grace is necessary to overcome temptations and to observe the Commandments, we must necessarily conclude that He gives all men, either immediately or mediately, actual grace to do good; and when mediately, no further grace is necessary to enable them to put into practice the means (such as prayer) of obtaining actual proximate grace. In another place, on the words of St. John's Gospel "No man cometh to me" etc., he says, "If the heart of man be not lifted up, it is from no defect on the part of Him who draws it, who as far as He is

[179] *De Lib. Arb.* 1. 3, c. 18.
[180] *De Nat. et Gr.* c. 67.
[181] *In Heb.* 12, lect. 3.
[182] *De Ver.* q. 14, a. 2.

concerned, never fails; but from an impediment caused by him who is being drawn."[183]

Scotus says the same: "God wills to save all men, so far as rests with Him, and with His antecedent will, by which He has given them the ordinary gifts necessary to salvation."[184] The Council of Cologne in 1536: "Although no one is converted except he is drawn by the Father, yet let no one pretend to excuse himself on the plea of not being drawn. He stands at the gate and knocks by the internal and the external Word."[185]

Testimony of Holy Scripture

Nor did the Fathers speak without warrant of the Holy Scriptures; for God in several places most clearly assures us that He does not neglect to assist us with His grace if we are willing to avail ourselves of it either for perseverance, if we are in a state of justification, or for conversion, if we are in sin.

"I stand at the gate and knock; if any man shall hear my voice and open to me the gate, I will come in to him" (Rev. 3:20). Bellarmine reasons well on this text, that Our Lord, who knows that man cannot open without His grace, would knock in vain at the door of his heart unless He had first conferred on him the grace to open when he will. This is exactly what St. Thomas teaches in explaining the text; he says that God gives everyone the grace necessary for salvation, that he may correspond to it if he will: "God by His most liberal will gives grace to every ne that prepares himself: Behold I stand at the door and knock. And therefore, the grace of God is wanting to no one, but communicates itself

---

[183] *In Jo.* 6, lect. 5.
[184] *In 1 Sent.* d. 46, q. un.
[185] P. 7, c. 32.

to all men, as far as it is concerned."[186] In another place, he says, "It is the business of God's Providence to provide everyone with what is necessary to salvation." So that, as St. Ambrose says: "The Lord knocks at the gate, because He truly wishes to enter; if He does not enter, or if after entering He does not remain in our souls, it is because we prevent Him from entering or drive Him out when He has entered. Because He comes and knocks at the door, He always wishes to enter; but it is through us that He does not always go in, nor always remain."[187]

"What is there that I ought to do more to my vineyard, that I have not done to it? Was it that I expected that it should bring forth grapes, and it hath brought forth wild grapes?" (Isa. 5:4). Bellarmine says on these words, "If He had not given the power to bring forth grapes, how could God say "expected"? And if God had not given to all men the grace necessary for salvation, He could not have said to the Jews, "What is there that I ought to have done more?" For they could have answered that if they had not yielded fruit, it was for lack of necessary assistance. Bellarmine says the same on the words of Our Lord: "How often would I have gathered together thy children ... and thou wouldst not" (Matt. 23:37). "How did He wish to be sought for by the unwilling, unless He helps them that they may be able to be willing?"

"We have received Thy mercy, O God, in the midst of Thy temple" (Ps. 47:10). On this St. Bernard observes: "Mercy is in the midst of the temple, not in any hole and corner, because there is no acceptance of persons with God; it is placed in public, it is offered to all, and no one is without it, except he who refuses it."

[186] *In Heb.* 12, lect. 3.
[187] *In Ps.* cxviii. s. 12.

"Or despisest thou the riches of His goodness, and patience, and long-suffering? Knowest thou not, that the benignity of God leadeth thee to penance?" (Rom. 2:4). You see that it is through his own malice that the sinner is not converted, because he despises the riches of the divine goodness which calls him and never ceases to move him to conversion by His grace. God hates sin but at the same time never ceases to love the sinful soul while it remains on earth and always gives it the assistance it requires for salvation: "But Thou sparest all, because they are Thine, O Lord, who lovest souls" (Wisd. 11:27). Hence we see, says Bellarmine, that God does not refuse grace to resist temptations to any sinner, however obstinate and blinded he may be: "Assistance to avoid new sin is always at hand for all men, either immediately or mediately (i.e., by means of prayer), so that they may ask further aid from God, by the help of which they will avoid sin."[188] Here we may quote what God says by Ezekiel: "As I live, saith the Lord God, I desire not the death of the wicked, but that the wicked turn from his way and live" (Ezek. 33:11). St. Peter says the same: "He beareth patiently for your sakes, not willing that any should perish, but that all should return to penance" (2 Pet. 3:9). If, therefore, God wishes that all should actually be converted, it must necessarily be held that He gives to all the grace which they need for actual conversion.

2. Obstinate or Hardened Sinners, and the Abandonment of Them by God

I know well that there are theologians who maintain that God refuses to certain obstinate sinners even sufficient grace. And, among others, they avail themselves of a position of St. Thomas,

---

[188] *De Gr. et Lib. Arb.* 1. 2, c. 7.

who says: "But although they who are in sin cannot through their own power avoid putting or interposing an obstacle to grace, unless they are prevented by grace, as we have shown; nevertheless, this also is imputed to them as a sin, because this defect is left in them from previous sin—as a drunken man is not excused from murder committed in that drunkenness which was incurred by his own fault. Besides, although he who is in sin has not this in his own power that he altogether avoid sin, yet he has power at this present moment to avoid this or that sin, as has been said; so that whatever he commits, he commits voluntarily; and therefore it is properly imputed to him as sin."[189] From this they gather that St. Thomas intends to say that sinners can indeed avoid particular sins, but not all sins, because in punishment for sins previously committed, they are deprived of all actual grace.

But we answer that here St. Thomas is not speaking of actual but of habitual or sanctifying grace, without which the sinner cannot keep himself long from falling into new sins, as he teaches in several places. And that he means the same in the passage just quoted is clear from the context.... Moreover, in the course of the chapter, he says: "For when the mind of man has declined from the state of uprightness, it is manifest that it has fallen from its relation, 'order' (*ordo*), to its true end.... Whensoever, therefore, anything shall have occurred to the mind conducive to the inordinate end, but improper for the true end, it will be chosen, unless the mind be brought back to its due relation, so as to prefer its true end to all others; and this is the effect of grace. But while anything repugnant to our last end is the object of our choice, it puts a hindrance in the way of the grace which conducts us to that end; whence it is manifest that, after

[189] *Contra Gent.* 1. 3, c. 160.

sinning, man cannot altogether abstain from sin before he is brought back by grace to the due order. And hence the opinion of the Pelagians is shown to be absurd, that man, being in sin, can without grace avoid (fresh) sin." And then he goes on with the sentence quoted above: "But although they," etc., of which our opponents make use.

So that, in the first place, the intention of St. Thomas is not to prove that some sinners are deprived of all actual grace, and therefore, being unable to avoid all sin, they do commit sin, and are worthy of punishment; but his intention is to prove against the Pelagians that a man who remains without sanctifying grace cannot abstain from sinning. And we see that he is here certainly speaking of sanctifying grace, for this is that which alone brings the soul back to the right order. It is of this same sanctifying grace that he intends to speak, when he says immediately after, "Except he be prevented by the assistance of grace"; by which he means that if the sinner is not prevented—that is, is not previously informed (*informato*)—by grace and brought back to the right order of holding God to be his last end, he cannot avoid committing fresh sins. And this is the meaning of the Thomists —for instance, of Ferrariensis (Silvestre) and Fr. Gonet—in their comments on this passage. But, without having recourse to other authors, it is quite clear from what St. Thomas himself says in his *Summa*, where he discusses the same point and brings forward the identical reasons in the same words as in the 160th chapter of his book *Contra Gentes*; and there he expressly says that he is only speaking of habitual or sanctifying grace.

And it is impossible that the holy Doctor could have meant otherwise, since he elsewhere teaches that, on the one hand, God's grace is never wanting to anyone, as he says in his commentary on St. John: "But lest you might suppose that this effect was consequent on the removal of the true light, the Evangelist, to obviate this opposition, adds, that was the true light which enlightens every man. For the Word enlightens, so far as He is concerned, because on His part He is wanting to no one but wishes all men to be saved. But if anyone is not enlightened, this is the fault of the man who turns himself away from the light that would enlighten him."[190] And, on the other hand, he teaches that there is no sinner so lost and abandoned by grace as not to be able to lay aside his obstinacy and to unite himself to the will of God, which he certainly cannot do without the assistance of grace: "During this life there is no man who cannot lay aside obstinacy of mind, and so conform to the divine will."[191] In another place he says, "So long as the use of free will remains to a man in this life ... he can prepare himself for grace by being sorry for his sins."[192] But no one can make an act of sorrow for sin without grace. In another place he says, "No man in this life can be so obstinate in evil but that it is possible for him to cooperate to his own deliverance."[193] "To cooperate" necessarily implies grace to cooperate with.

In another place he observes, on the text of St. Paul, "He wills all to be saved." "Therefore, the grace of God is wanting to no man; but, as far as it is concerned, it communicates itself to all." Again, on the same words, "God, so far as He is concerned, is prepared to give grace to all men.... Those, therefore, only are deprived of grace who permit a hindrance to grace to exist in themselves; and, therefore, they cannot be excused if they

---

[190] *In Jo.* i. lect. 5.
[191] *In 1 Sent.* d. 48, q. I, a. 3.
[192] *In 4 Sent.* d. 20, q. I, a. I.
[193] *De Ver.* q. 24, a. II.

sin."[194] And when St. Thomas says, "God is prepared to give grace to all," he does not mean actual grace, but only sanctifying grace.

Cardinal Gotti justly contradicts those who say that God keeps ready at hand the aids necessary for salvation but in matter of fact does not give them to all. Of what use would it be to a sick man (says this learned author) if the physician only kept the remedies ready and then would not apply them? Then he concludes (quite to the point of our argument) that we must necessarily say, "God not only offers but also confers on every individual, even on infidels and hardened sinners, help sufficient to observe the Commandments, whether it be proximate or remote."[195]

For the rest, St. Thomas says that it is only the sins of the devils and the damned that cannot be wiped out by penance; but, on the other hand, "to say that there is any sin in this life of which a man cannot repent is erroneous ... because this doctrine would derogate from the power of grace" (III, q. 86, art. 1). If grace were wanting to anyone, certainly he could not repent. Moreover, as we have already seen, St. Thomas expressly teaches in several places, and especially in his comment on Hebrews 12, that God, as far as He is concerned, refuses to no man the grace necessary for conversion: "The grace of God is wanting to no man; but, as far as it is concerned, communicates itself to all." So that the learned author of the Theology for the use of the seminary of Peterkau says, "It is a calumny to impute to St. Thomas that he taught that any sinners were totally deserted by God."[196]

---

[194] *Contra Gent.* 1.3, c. 159.
[195] *De Div.* Vol. q. 2, d. 3, § 2.
[196] *Lib.* 3, c. 3, q. 4.

Prayer

Bellarmine makes a sound distinction on this point and says that for avoiding fresh sins every sinner has at all times sufficient assistance, at least mediately: "The necessary and sufficient assistance for the avoidance of sin is given by God's goodness to all men at all times, either immediately or mediately.... We say *or mediately* because it is certain that some men have not that help by which they can immediately avoid sin, but yet have the help which enables them to obtain from God greater safeguards, by the assistance of which they will avoid sins."[197] But for the grace of conversion, he says that this is not given at all times to the sinner; but that no one will be ever so far left to himself "as to be surely and absolutely deprived of God's help through all this life, so as to have cause to despair of salvation."[198]

And so says the theologians who follow St. Thomas — thus Soto: "I am absolutely certain, and I believe that all the holy Doctors who are worthy of the name were always most positive, that no one was ever deserted by God in this mortal life."[199] And the reason is evident; for if the sinner was quite abandoned by grace, either his sins afterward committed could no longer be imputed to him, or he would be under an obligation to do that which he had no power to fulfill; but it is a positive rule of St. Augustine that there is never a sin in that which cannot be avoided: "No one sins in that which can by no means be avoided."[200] And this is agreeable to the teaching of the Apostle: "God is faithful, who will not suffer you to be tempted above that which you are able; but will also make with the temptation

[197] *De Gr. et Lib. Arb.* 1. 2, c. 7.
[198] Ibid. c. 6.
[199] *De Nat. et Gr.* 1. I, c. 18.
[200] *De Lib. Arb.* l.3 c. 18.

issue, that you may be able to bear it" (1 Cor. 10:13). The word "issue" means the divine assistance, which God always gives to the tempted to enable them to resist, as St. Cyprian explains it: "He will make with the temptation a way of escape."[201] And Primasius more clearly: "He will so order the issue that we shall be able to endure; that is, in temptation He will strengthen you with the help of His grace, so that ye may be able to bear it." St. Augustine and St. Thomas go so far as to say that God would be unjust and cruel if He obliged anyone to a command which he could not keep. St. Augustine says, "It is the deepest injustice to reckon anyone guilty of sin for not doing that which he could not do."[202] And St. Thomas: "God is not more cruel than man; but it is reckoned cruelty in a man to oblige a person by law to do that which he cannot fulfill; therefore we must by no means imagine this of God."[203] "It is, however, different," he says, "when it is through his own neglect that he has not the grace to be able to keep the Commandments,"[204] which properly means, when man neglects to avail himself of the remote grace of prayer, in order to obtain the proximate grace to enable him to keep the law, as the Council of Trent teaches: "God does not command impossibilities; but by commanding admonishes you to do what you can, and to ask for that which is beyond your power; and by His help enables you to do it."[205]

St. Augustine repeats his decision in many other places that there is no sin in what cannot be avoided. In one he says,

---

[201] *Testim.* 1. 3. n. 91.
[202] *De Duab. An.* c. 12.
[203] *In 2 Sent.* d. 28, q. 1, a. 3.
[204] *De Ver.* q. 24, a. 14.
[205] Session 6, Cap. 11.

"Whether there be iniquity or whether there be justice, if it was not in the man's power, there can be no just reward, no just punishment."[206] Elsewhere he says, "Finally, if no power is given them to abstain from their works, we cannot hold that they sin."[207] Again, "The devil, indeed, suggests; but with the help of God it is in our power to choose or to refuse his suggestions. And so, when by God's help it is in your power, why do you not rather determine to obey God than him?"[208] Again, "No one, therefore, is answerable for what he has not received."[209] Again, "No one is worthy of blame for not doing that which he cannot do."[210]

Other Fathers have taught the same doctrine. So St. Jerome: "We are not forced by necessity to be either virtuous or vicious; for where there is necessity, there is neither condemnation nor crown."[211] Tertullian: "For a law would not be given to him who had it not in his power to observe it duly."[212] Marcus the Hermit: "Hidden grace assists us; but it depends on us to do or not to do good according to our strength."[213] So also St. Irenaeus, St. Cyril of Alexandria, St. Chrysostom, and others.

Nor is there any difficulty in what St. Thomas says, that grace is denied to some persons, in punishment of Original Sin: "To whomsoever the assistance of grace is given, it is given through simple mercy; but from those to whom it is not given, it is withheld justly in punishment of previous sin, or at least of Original

---

[206] *Cont. Faüst.* 1. 22, c. 78.
[207] *De Duab. An.* c. 12.
[208] Sermon 253, E. B. App.
[209] *De Lib. Arb.* l. 3, c. 16.
[210] *De Duab. An.* c. II.
[211] Cont. Jov. 1. 2.
[212] *Cont. Marcion.* 1. 2.
[213] *De Just, ex op.* c. 56.

Sin, as Augustine says."[214] For, as Cardinal Gotti well observes, St. Augustine and St. Thomas are speaking of actual proximate grace to satisfy the precepts of faith and charity, of which, indeed, St. Thomas is speaking in this place; but, for all this, they do not intend to deny that God gives every man interior grace, by means of which he may at any rate obtain by prayer the grace of faith, and of salvation; since, as we have already seen, these holy Doctors do not doubt that God grants to every man at least remote grace to satisfy the precepts. Here we may add the authority of St. Prosper, who says, "All men enjoy some measure of Heavenly teaching; and though the measure of grace be small, it is sufficient to be a remedy for some, and to be a testimony for all."[215]

Nor could it be understood otherwise; for if it were true that any had sinned for want of even remote sufficient grace, withheld through Original Sin being imputed to them as a fault, it would follow that the liberty of will, which by a figure of speech we are said to have had in the sin of Adam, would be sufficient to make us actual sinners. But this cannot be said, as it is expressly condemned in the first proposition of Michael Baius, who said, "That liberty which caused sin to be voluntary and free in its cause—namely, in Original Sin, and in the liberty of Adam when sinning—is sufficient to (cause) formal sin (in us), and to make us deserve punishment." Against this proposition we may make use of what Bellarmine said, that to commit a personal sin distinct from the sin of Adam, a new exertion of free will is requisite, and a free will distinct from that of Adam; otherwise there is no distinct sin; according to the doctrine of St. Thomas, who teaches, "For a personal sin, absolute personal liberty is requisite." Further, with

---

[214] II-II, q. 2, art. 5.—*August. De Corr. et Grat.* c. II.
[215] *De Voc. Gent.* l. 2, c. 15.

respect to the Baptized, the Council of Trent has declared that in them there remains nothing to condemn: "God hates nothing in the regenerate; for there is no condemnation to them who are truly buried with Christ by Baptism unto death." And it is added that concupiscence is not left in us as a punishment, "but for our trial; and it cannot harm those who do not consent to it."[216] On the contrary, the concupiscence left in us would do exceedingly great harm to man, if, on account of it, God denied him even the remote grace necessary to obtain salvation.

From all this, several theologians conclude that to say that God refuses to anyone sufficient help to enable him to keep the Commandments would be contrary to the faith, because in that case God would oblige us to impossibilities.

... This doctrine, that a man, when fallen, sins, not having liberty to do otherwise than to choose what sin he will commit, and is necessitated to commit some sin, justly offends Msgr. de Saleon, archbishop of Vienna, who, in his book *Jansenismus Redivivus*, writes as follows: "Who will endure to hear that a man once fallen, being deprived of grace, can enjoy no other liberty than that of choosing one sin rather than another, being necessitated to sin in some way?"[217] So that a criminal condemned to death, who has no other liberty allowed him than to choose whether he will die by the sword, by poison, or by fire, may be said, when he has made his choice, to die a voluntary and free death. And how can sin be imputed to a man who might sin in some way or another? The sixty-seventh of the condemned Propositions of Baius is as follows: "Man sins damnably even in that which he does through necessity." How can there be

---

[216] Sess. 5. De Pecc. or. n. 5.
[217] P. 2, a. 6.

liberty, where there is necessity to sin? Jansenius answers that the liberty of will, which by a figure of speech we are said to have had in Adam's sin, is sufficient to make us sinners. But this too was condemned in Baius's first proposition, "That liberty" etc., as we have seen above.

… In the Holy Scriptures God is often said to do what He only permits; so that if we would not blaspheme with Calvin, and say that God positively destines and determines some persons to sin, we must say that God permits some sinners, in penalty of their faults, to be, on the one hand, assailed by vehement temptations, which is the evil from which we pray God to deliver us when we say, "Lead us not into temptation"; and, on the other hand, that they remain morally abandoned in their sin, so that their conversion, and the resistance they should make to temptation, although neither impossible nor desperate, is yet, through their faults and their bad habits, very difficult; since, in their laxity of life, they have only very rare and weak desires and motions to resist their bad habit and to regain the way of salvation. And this the imperfect obstinacy of the hardened sinner which St. Thomas describes: "He is hardened who cannot easily cooperate in his escape from sin and this is imperfect obstinacy, because a man may be obstinate in this life, if he has a will so fixed upon sin, that no motions towards arise, except very weak ones."[218] On the one side, the mind is obscured, the will is hardened against God's inspirations, and attached to the pleasures of sense, so as to despise and feel disgust for spiritual blessings; the sensual passions and appetites reign in the soul through the bad habits that have been acquired; on the other side, the illuminations and the callings of God are, by its own fault, rendered scarcely efficacious

[218] *De Ver.* q. 24, a. II.

to move the soul, which has so despised them and made so bad a use of them, that it even feels a certain aversion toward them, because it does not want to be disturbed in its sensual gratifications. All these things constitute moral abandonment; and when a sinner has once fallen into it, it is only with the utmost difficulty that he can escape from his miserable state and bring himself to live a well-regulated life.

In order to escape and pass at once from such disorder to a state of salvation, a great and extraordinary grace would be requisite; but God seldom confers such a grace on these obstinate sinners. Sometimes He gives it, says St. Thomas, and chooses them for vessels of mercy; as the Apostle calls them, in order to make known His goodness; but to the rest He justly refuses it, and leaves them in their unhappy state, in order to show forth His justice and power:

"Sometimes," says the Angel of the Schools, "out of the abundance of His goodness He prevents with His assistance even those who put a hindrance in the way of His grace, and converts them. And as He does not enlighten all the blind, nor cure all the sick, so neither does He assist all who place an impediment to His grace, so as to convert them." This is what the Apostle means when he says that God, "to show forth His anger, and to make His power known, endured with much patience, vessels of wrath, fitted for destruction, that He might show the riches of His glory upon the vessels of mercy, which He hath prepared unto glory" (Rom. 9:22–23). Then he adds, "But since out of the number of those who are involved in the same sins, there are some to whom God gives the grace of conversion, while others He only endures, or allows to go on in the course of things, we are not to inquire the reason why He converts some and not others." For the Apostle says, "Has not the potter power over the clay, to make of the same mass one vessel to honor; and another to dishonor?" (Rom. 9: 21).[219]

We do not then deny (to bring this point to a conclusion) that there is such a thing as the moral abandonment of some obstinate sinners, so that their conversion is morally impossible; that is to say, very difficult. And this concession is abundantly sufficient for the laudable object which our opponents have in defending their opinion, which is to restrain evildoers and to induce them to consider, before they come to fall into such a deplorable state. But then it is cruelty (as Petrocorensis well says) to take from them all hope, and entirely to shut against them the way of salvation, by the doctrine that they have fallen into so complete an abandonment as to be deprived of all actual grace to enable them to avoid fresh sins and to be converted; at any rate, mediately by means of prayer (which is not refused to any man while he lives ...), whereby they can afterward obtain abundant help for placing themselves in a state of salvation: since the fear of total abandonment would lead them not only to despair but also to give themselves more completely to their vices, in the belief that they are altogether destitute of grace; so that they have no hope left of escaping eternal damnation.

[219] *Cont. Gent.* 1. 3, c. 161.

Part III

Mental Prayer

Chapter 1

Mental Prayer Is Morally Necessary for Salvation

1. Mental Prayer Enlightens the Mind

In the first place, without mental prayer, the soul is without light. They, says St. Augustine, who keep their eyes shut cannot see the way to their country. The eternal truths are all spiritual things that are seen not with eyes of the body but with the eyes of the mind; that is, by reflection and consideration. Now, they who do not make mental prayer do not see these truths, neither do they see the importance of eternal salvation and the means which they can adopt in order to obtain it. The loss of so many souls arises from the neglect of considering the great affair of our salvation and what we must do in order to be saved. "With desolation," says the prophet Jeremiah, "is all the land made desolate: because there is none that considereth in the heart" (Jer. 12:11). On the other hand, the Lord says that he who keeps before his eyes the truths of faith—that is, death, judgment, and the happy or unhappy eternity that awaits us—shall never fall into sin. "In all thy works remember thy last end, and thou shalt never sin" (Eccles. 7:40).

Prayer

St. Bonaventure also says that mental prayer is, as it were, a mirror, in which we see all the stains of the soul. In a letter to the bishop of Osma, St. Teresa says, "Although it appears to us that we have no imperfections, still when God opens the eyes of the soul, as He usually does in prayer, our imperfections are then clearly seen." He who does not make mental prayer does not even know his defects, and therefore, as St. Bernard says, he does not abhor them. He does not even know the dangers to which his eternal salvation is exposed, and, therefore, he does not even think of avoiding them. But he who applies himself to meditation instantly sees his faults, and the dangers of perdition, and, seeing them, he will reflect on the remedies for them. By meditating on eternity, David was excited to the practice of virtue and to sorrow and works of penance for his sins. "I thought upon the days of old, and I had in my mind the eternal years. And I meditated in the night with my own heart: and I was exercised and I swept my spirit" (Ps. 76:6). When the soul, like the solitary turtle, retires and recollects itself in meditation to converse with God, then the flowers — that is, good desires — appear; then comes the time of pruning — that is, the correction of faults which are discovered in mental prayer. "Consider," says St. Bernard, "that the time of pruning is at hand, if the time of meditation has gone before."[220] For (says the saint in another place) meditation regulates the affections, directs the actions, and corrects defects.

2. Mental Prayer Disposes the Heart to the Practice of Virtues

Moreover, without meditation there is not strength to resist the temptations of our enemies, and to practice the virtues of the Gospel.

[220] *De Cons.* L. 2, c. 6.

Meditation is like fire with regard to iron, which, when cold, is hard and can be wrought only with difficulty. But placed in the fire, it becomes soft, and the workman gives it any form he wishes, says the venerable Bartholomew à Martyribus. To observe the divine precepts and counsels, it is necessary to have a tender heart, that is, a heart docile and prepared to receive the impressions of celestial inspirations, and ready to obey them. It was this that Solomon asked of God: "Give, therefore, to thy servant an understanding heart" (3 Kings 3:9). Sin has made our heart hard and indocile; for, being altogether inclined to sensual pleasure, it resists, as the Apostle complained, the laws of the spirit: "But I see another law in my members, fighting against the law of my mind" (Rom. 7:23).

But man becomes docile and tender to the influence of grace which is communicated in mental prayer. By the contemplation of the divine goodness, the great love which God has borne him, and the immense benefits which God has bestowed upon him, man is inflamed with love, his heart is softened, and made obedient to the divine inspirations. But without mental prayer his heart will remain hard and restive and disobedient, and thus he will be lost: "A hard heart shall fare evil at the last" (Eccles. 3:27). Hence, St. Bernard exhorted Pope Eugene never to omit meditations on account of external occupations. "I fear for you, O Eugene, lest the multitude of affairs (prayer and consideration being intermitted) may bring you to a hard heart, which abhors not itself, because it perceives not."[221]

Some may imagine that the long time which devout souls give to prayer, and which they could spend in useful works, is unprofitable and lost time. But such persons know not that in

---

[221] *De Cons.* 1. I, c. 2.

mental prayer souls acquire strength to conquer enemies and to practice virtue. "From this leisure," says St. Bernard, "strength comes forth." Hence, the Lord commanded that His spouse should not be disturbed. "I adjure you ... that you stir not up nor awake my beloved till she please" (Song of Sol. 3:5). He says, "till she please," for the sleep or repose which the soul takes in mental prayer is perfectly voluntary but is, at the same time, necessary for its spiritual life. He who does not sleep has not strength to work nor to walk, but goes tottering along the way. The soul that does not repose and acquire strength in meditation is not able to resist temptations, and totters on the road. In the life of the Venerable Sr. Mary Crucified, we read that, while at prayer, she heard a devil boasting that he had made a nun omit the common meditation and that afterward, because he continued to tempt her, she was in danger of consenting to mortal sin. The servant of God ran to the nun, and, with the divine aid, rescued her from the criminal suggestion. Behold the danger to which one who omits meditation exposes his soul! St. Teresa used to say that he who neglects mental prayer needs not a devil to carry him to Hell but that he brings himself there with his own hands. And the Abbot Diodes says that "the man who omits mental prayer soon becomes either a beast or a devil."

3. Mental Prayers Helps Us to Pray as We Should

Without petitions on our part, God does not grant the divine helps; and without aid from God, we cannot observe the Commandments. From the absolute necessity of the prayer of petition arises the moral necessity of mental prayer; for he who neglects meditation and is distracted with worldly affairs will not know his spiritual wants, the dangers to which his salvation is exposed, the means which he must adopt in order to conquer temptations, or even the necessity of the prayer of petition for all men; thus, he will give up the practice of prayer, and by neglecting to ask God's graces he will certainly be lost. The great Bishop Palafox, in his annotations to the letters of St. Teresa, says: "How can charity last, unless God gives perseverance? How will the Lord give us perseverance, if we neglect to ask Him for it? And how shall we ask Him without mental prayer? Without mental prayer, there is not the communication with God which is necessary for the preservation of virtue."[222] And Cardinal Bellarmine says that for him who neglects meditation, it is morally impossible to live without sin.

Someone may say: I do not make mental prayer, but I say many vocal prayers. But it is necessary to know, as St. Augustine remarks, that to obtain the divine grace, it is not enough to pray with the tongue; it is necessary also to pray with the heart. On the words of David "I cried to the Lord with my voice" (Ps. 141:2), the holy Doctor says, "Many cry not with their own voice (that is, not with the interior voice of the soul), but with that of the body. Your thoughts are a cry to the Lord. Cry within, where God hears."[223] This is what the Apostle inculcates: "Praying at all times in the spirit" (Eph. 6:18). In general, vocal prayers are said distractedly with the voice of the body, but not of the heart, especially when they are long, and still more especially when said by a person who does not make mental prayer; and, therefore, God seldom hears them and seldom grants the graces asked. Many say the Rosary, the Office of the Blessed Virgin, and perform other works of devotion; but they still continue in sin. But it is impossible for him who perseveres in mental prayer to

[222] Letter 8.
[223] *In Ps.* xxx. en. 4.

Prayer

continue in sin: he will either give up meditation or renounce sin. A great servant of God used to say that mental prayer and sin cannot exist together. And this we see by experience; they who make mental prayer rarely incur the enmity of God; and should they ever have the misfortune of falling into sin, by persevering in mental prayer they see their misery and return to God. Let a soul, says St. Teresa, be ever so negligent, if it perseveres in meditation, the Lord will bring it back to the haven of salvation.

Chapter 2

⊶ ⬦•⬧•⬦ ⊷

Mental Prayer Is Indispensable in Order to Attain Perfection

All the saints have become saints by mental prayer. Mental prayer is the blessed furnace in which souls are inflamed with the divine love. "In my meditation," says David, "a fire shall flame out" (Ps. 38:4). St. Vincent of Paul used to say that it would be a miracle if a sinner who attends the sermons in the mission, or in the spiritual exercises, were not converted. Now, he who preaches and speaks in the exercises is only a man; but it is God Himself who speaks to the soul in meditation. "I will lead her into the wilderness; and I will speak to her heart" (Hos. 2:14). St. Catherine of Bologna used to say, "He who does not practice mental prayer deprives himself of the bond that unites the soul with God; hence, finding her alone, the devil will easily make her his own." "How", she would say, "can I conceive that the love of God is found in the soul that cares but little to treat with God in prayer?"

Where but in meditation have the saints been inflamed with divine love? By means of mental prayer, St. Peter of Alcantara was inflamed to such a degree that in order to cool himself, he ran into a frozen pool, and the frozen water began to boil like water in a caldron placed on the fire. In mental prayer, St. Philip

Prayer

Neri became inflamed and trembled so that he shook the entire room. In mental prayer, St. Aloysius Gonzaga was so inflamed with divine ardor that his very face appeared to be on fire, and his heart beat as strongly as if it wished to fly from the body.

St. Laurence Justinian says: "By the efficacy of mental prayer, temptation is banished, sadness is driven away, lost virtue is restored, fervor which has grown cold is excited, and the lovely flame of divine love is augmented."[224] Hence, St. Aloysius Gonzaga has justly said that he who does not make much mental prayer will never attain a high degree of perfection.

A man of prayer, says David, is like a tree planted near the current of waters, which brings forth fruit in due time; all his actions prosper before God. "Blessed is the man … who shall meditate on His law, day and night! And he shall be like a tree which is planted near the running waters, which shall bring forth its fruit in due season, and his leaf shall not fall off: and all whatsoever he shall do shall prosper" (Ps. 1:1–3). Mark the words "in due season"; that is, at the time when he ought to bear such a pain, such an affront, etc.

St. John Chrysostom compared mental prayer to a fountain in the middle of a garden. Oh, what an abundance of flowers and verdant plants do we see in the garden which is always refreshed with water from the fountain! Such, precisely is the soul that practices mental prayer; you will see that it always advances in good desires and that it always brings forth more abundant fruits of virtue. Whence does the soul receive so many blessings? From meditation, by which it is continually irrigated. "Thy plants are a Paradise of pomegranates with the fruits of the orchard. … The fountain of gardens, the well of living waters, which run with

---

[224] *De Casto Conn.* c. 22.

a strong stream from Libanus" (Song of Sol. 4:13, 15). But let the fountain cease to water the garden, and, behold, the flowers, plants, and all instantly wither away; and why? Because the water has failed. You will see that as long as such a person makes mental prayer, he is modest, humble, devout, and mortified in all things. But let him omit meditation, and you will instantly find him wanting in modesty of the eyes, proud, resenting every word, indevout, no longer frequenting the Sacraments and the church; you will find him attached to vanity, to useless conversations, to pastimes, and to earthly pleasures; and why? The water has failed, and, therefore, fervor has ceased. "My soul is as earth without water unto thee.... My spirit hath fainted away" (Ps. 142:6–7). The soul has neglected mental prayer; the garden is therefore dried up, and the miserable soul goes from bad to worse. When a soul abandons meditation, St. Chrysostom regards it not only as sick but as dead. "He," says the holy Doctor, "who prays not to God, nor desires to enjoy assiduously His divine conversation, is dead.... The death of a soul is not to be prostrated before God."[225]

The same Father says that mental prayer is the root of the fruitful vine. And St. John Climacus writes that prayer is a bulwark against the assault of afflictions, the spring of virtues, the procurer of graces. Rufinus asserts that all the spiritual progress of the soul flows from mental prayer. And Gerson goes so far as to say that he who neglects meditation cannot, without a miracle, lead the life of a Christian. Speaking of mental prayer, Jeremiah says, "He shall sit solitary, and hold his peace; because he hath taken it up upon himself" (Lam. 3:28). That is, a soul cannot have a relish for God unless it withdraws from creatures and sits, that is, stops to contemplate the goodness, the love, the amiableness

[225] *De or.* D. 1. I.

of God. But when solitary and recollected in meditation — that is, when it takes away its thoughts from the world — it is then raised above itself and departs from prayer very different from what it was when it began it.

St. Ignatius of Loyola used to say that mental prayer is the short way to attain perfection. In a word, he who advances most in meditation makes the greatest progress in perfection. In mental prayer, the soul is filled with holy thoughts, with holy affections, desires, and holy resolutions, and with love for God. There man sacrifices his passions, his appetites, his earthly attachments, and all the interests of self-love. Moreover, by praying for them, in mental prayer we can save many sinners, as was done by St. Teresa and St. Mary Magdalene de Pazzi and is done by all souls enamored of God, who never omit, in their meditations, to recommend to Him all infidels, heretics, and all poor sinners, begging Him also to give zeal to priests who work in His vineyard, that they may convert His enemies. In mental prayer we can also, by the sole desire of performing them, gain the merit of many good works which we do not perform. For, as the Lord punishes bad desires, so, on the other hand, He rewards all our good desires.

Prayer

My Jesus, Thou has loved me in the midst of pains; and in the midst of sufferings, I wish to love Thee. Thou has spared nothing, Thou hast even given Thy blood and Thy life, in order to gain my love; and shall I continue, as hitherto, to be reserved in loving Thee? No, my Redeemer, it shall not be so: the ingratitude with which I have hitherto treated Thee is sufficient. To Thee I consecrate my whole heart. Thou alone dost deserve all my love. Thee alone do I wish to love. My God, since

Thou wishest me to be entirely Thine, give me strength to serve Thee as Thou deservest, during the remainder of my life. Pardon my tepidity and my past infidelities. How often have I omitted mental prayer, in order to indulge my caprice! Alas, how often, when it was in my power to remain with Thee in order to please Thee, have I remained with creatures, so as to offend Thee! Oh, that so many lost years would return! But, since they will not return, the remaining days of my life must be entirely Thine, O my beloved Lord! I love Thee, O my Jesus! I love Thee, O my Sovereign Good! Thou art and shall be forever the only love of my soul.

O Mother of fair love, O Mary! Obtain for me the grace to love thy Son and to spend the remainder of my life in His love. Thou dost obtain from Jesus whatsoever thou wishest. Through thy prayer I hope for this gift.

Chapter 3

⊷ ⊷•⊷ ⊷

The Ends of Mental Prayer

In order to practice well mental prayer, or meditation, and to make it truly profitable to the soul, we must well ascertain the ends for which we attempt it.

To Unite Ourselves to God

We must meditate in order to unite ourselves more completely to God. It is not so much good thoughts in the intellect as good acts of the will, or holy desires, that unite us to God; and such are the acts which we perform in meditation — acts of humility, confidence, self-sacrifice, resignation, and especially of love and of repentance for our sins. Acts of love, says St. Teresa, are those that keep the soul inflamed with holy love.

But the perfection of this love consists in making our will one with that of God; for the chief effect of love, as Dionysius the Areopagite says, is to unite the wills of those who love, so that they have but one heart and one will. St. Teresa also says, "All that he who exercises himself in prayer should aim at is to conform himself to the divine will, and he may be assured that in this consists the highest perfection; he who best practices this will receive the greatest gifts from God and will make the greatest progress in an interior life."[226]

There are many, however, who complain that they go to prayer and do not find God, the reason of which is that they carry with them a heart full of earth. "Detach the heart from creatures," says St. Teresa; "seek God, and you will find Him." "The Lord is good to them that hope in Him, to the soul that seeketh Him" (Lam. 3:25). Therefore, to find God in prayer, the soul must be stripped of its love for the things of earth, and then God will speak to it: "I will lead her into the wilderness, and I will speak to her heart" (Hos. 2:14). But in order to find God, solitude of the body, as St. Gregory observes, is not enough; that of the heart is necessary too. The Lord one day said to St. Teresa: "I would willingly speak to many souls; but the world makes such a noise in their heart that my voice cannot make itself heard." Ah! When a detached soul is engaged in prayer, truly does God speak to it and make it understand the love which He has borne it; and then the soul, says St. Laurence Justinian, burning with holy love, speaks not; but in that silence, oh, how much does it say! The silence of charity, observes the same writer, says more to God than could be said by the utmost powers of human elo-quence; each sigh that it utters is a manifestation of its whole interior. It then seems as if it could not repeat often enough, "My Beloved to me, and I to Him."

To Obtain Grace from God

We must meditate in order to obtain from God the graces that are necessary to advance in the way of salvation, and especially to avoid sin, and to use the means which will lead us to perfection.

---

[226] *Interior Castle*, d. 2, ch. I.

The best fruit that comes from meditation is the exercise of prayer. Almighty God, ordinarily speaking, does not give grace to any but those who pray. St. Gregory writes: "God desires to be entreated; He desires to be constrained; He desires to be, as it were, conquered by importunity." It is true that at all times the Lord is ready to hear us, but at the time of meditation, when we are most truly in converse with God, He is most bountiful in giving us His aid.

Above all, should we, in meditation, ask God for perseverance and His holy love.

Final perseverance is not a single grace, but a chain of graces, to which must correspond the chain of our prayers. If we cease to pray, God will cease to give us His help, and we shall perish. He who does not practice meditation will find the greatest difficulty in persevering in grace till death. Let us remember what Palafox says: "How will the Lord give us perseverance if we do not ask it? And how shall we ask for it without meditation? Without meditation there is no communion with God."

We must also be urgent with prayers to obtain from God His holy love. St. Francis de Sales says that all virtues come in union with holy love. "All good things came to me together with her" (Wisd. 7:7).

Let us, therefore, pray continually for perseverance and love; and, in order to pray with greater confidence, let us ever bear in mind the promise made us by Jesus Christ, that whatever we seek from God through the merits of His Son, He will give it to us. Let us, then, pray, and pray always, if we would that God should make us abound in every blessing. Let us pray for ourselves, and, if we have zeal for the glory of God, let us pray also for others. It is a thing most pleasing to God to be entreated for unbelievers and heretics, and all sinners. "Let the people, O God, confess to Thee" (Ps. 66:6). Let us say, O Lord, make them know Thee, make them love Thee. We read in the lives of St. Teresa and St. Mary Magdalene of Pazzi how God inspired these holy women to pray for sinners. And to prayer for sinners let us also add prayers for the holy souls in Purgatory.

We Ought Not to Seek in Mental Prayer Spiritual Consolations

We must apply ourselves to meditation not for the sake of spiritual consolations but chiefly in order to learn what is the will of God concerning us. "Speak Lord," said Samuel to God, "for Thy servant heareth" (1 Sam. 3:9). Lord, make me to know what Thou wilt, that I may do it. Some persons continue meditation as long as consolations continue; but when these cease, they leave off meditation. It is true that God is accustomed to comfort His beloved souls at the time of meditation and to give them some foretaste of the delights He prepares in Heaven for those who love Him. These are things which the lovers of the world do not comprehend; they who have not taste except for earthly delights despise those which are celestial. Oh, if they were wise, how surely would they leave their pleasures to shut themselves in their closets, to speak alone with God! Meditation is nothing more than a converse between the soul and God; the soul pours forth to Him its affections, its desires, its fears, its requests, and God speaks to the heart, causing it to know His goodness and the love which He bears it and what it must do to please Him.

But these delights are not constant, and for the most part, holy souls experience much dryness of spirit in meditation. "With dryness and temptations," says St. Teresa, "the Lord makes proof of those who love Him." And she adds, "Even if this dryness lasts through life, let not the soul leave off meditation; the time will come when all will be well rewarded." The time of dryness is the time for gaining the greatest rewards; and when we find ourselves apparently without fervor, without good desires, and, as it were, unable to do a good act, let us humble ourselves and resign ourselves, for this very meditation will be more fruitful than others. It is enough then to say, if we can say nothing more, "O Lord, help me, have mercy on me, abandon me not!" Let us also have recourse to our comforter, the most holy Mary. Happy he who does not leave off meditation in the hour of desolation.

Chapter 4

Principal Subjects of Meditation

The Holy Spirit says, "In all thy works remember thy last end, and thou shalt never sin" (Eccles. 7:40). He who often meditates on the four last things—namely, death, judgment, and the eternity of Hell and Paradise—will not fall into sin. But these truths are not seen with the eye of the body; only the soul perceives them. If they are not meditated on, they vanish from the mind; and then the pleasures of the senses present themselves, and those who do not keep before themselves the eternal truths are easily taken up by them; and this is the reason why so many abandon themselves to vice and are damned. All Christians know and believe that they must die, and that we shall all be judged; but because they do not think about this, they will live far away from God.

If we, moreover, do not meditate especially on our obligation to love God on account of His infinite perfections and the great blessings that He has conferred upon us, and the love that He has borne us, we shall hardly detach ourselves from the love of creatures in order to fix our whole love on God. It is in the time of prayer that God gives us to understand the worthlessness of earthly things, and the value of the good things of Heaven; and then it is that He inflames with His love those hearts that do not offer resistance to His calls.

After all, the good rule is that we preferably meditate on the truths and mysteries that touch us more and procure for our soul the most abundant nourishment. Yet the subject most suitable for a person who aspires to perfection ought to be the Passion of Our Lord. Louis Blosius relates that Our Lord revealed to several holy women — to St. Gertrude, St. Bridget, St. Mechtilde, and St. Catherine of Siena — that they who meditate on His Passion are very dear to Him. According to St. Francis de Sales, the Passion of Our Redeemer should be the ordinary subject of the meditation of every Christian. Oh, what an excellent book is the Passion of Jesus! There we understand, better than in any other book, the malice of sin and also the mercy and love of God for man. To me it appears that Jesus Christ has suffered so many different pains — the Scourging, the Crowning with thorns, the Crucifixion, etc. — that, having before our eyes so many painful mysteries, we might have a variety of different subjects for meditating on His Passion, by which we might excite sentiments of gratitude and love.

Chapter 5

The Place and Time
Suitable for Meditation

The Place

We can meditate in every place, at home or elsewhere, even in walking and in working. How many are there who, not being able to do so otherwise, raise their hearts to God and apply their minds to mental prayer without leaving for this purpose their occupations, their work, or meditate even when traveling! He who seeks God will find Him everywhere at all times.

The essential condition to converse with God is the solitude of the heart, without which prayer would be worthless, and, as St. Gregory says, it would profit us little or nothing to be with the body in a solitary place, while the heart is full of worldly thoughts and affections. But to enjoy the solitude of the heart, which consists in being disengaged from worldly thoughts and affections, deserts and caves are not absolutely necessary. Those who from necessity are obliged to converse with the world, whenever their hearts are free from worldly attachments, even in the public streets, in places of resort, and public assemblies, can possess a solitude of heart and continue united with God. All those occupations that we undertake in order to fulfill the divine will have no power to prevent the solitude of the heart. St. Catherine of Siena truly found God in the midst of the household labors in which her parents kept her employed in order to draw her from devotional exercises; but in the midst of these affairs, she preserved a retirement in her heart, which she called her cell, and there ceased not to converse with God alone.

However, when we can, we should retire to a solitary place to make our meditation. Our Lord has said, "When thou shalt pray, enter thy chamber, and, having shut the door, pray to thy Father in secret" (Matt. 6:6). St. Bernard says that silence, and the absence of all noise, almost force the soul to think of the goods of Heaven.

But the best place for making mental prayer is the church; for Jesus Christ especially delights in the meditation that is made before the Blessed Sacrament, since there it appears that He bestows light and grace most abundantly upon those who visit Him. He has left Himself in this Sacrament, not only to be the food of souls that receive Him in Holy Communion but also to be found at all times by everyone who seeks Him. Devout pilgrims go to the holy House of Loreto, where Jesus Christ dwelt during His life; and to Jerusalem, where He died on the Cross; but how much greater ought to be our devotion when we find Him before us in the tabernacle, in which this Lord Himself now dwells in person, who lived among us and died for us on Calvary! It is not permitted in the world for persons of all ranks to speak alone with kings; but with Jesus Christ, the King of Kings, both nobles and plebeians, rich and poor, can converse at their will, setting before Him their wants, and seeking His grace; and there Jesus gives audience to all, hears all, and comforts all.

The Time

We have here to consider two things—namely, the time of the day most suitable for mental prayer and the time to be spent in making it.

1. According to St. Bonaventure, the morning and the evening are the two parts of the day which, ordinarily speaking, are the fittest for meditation. But, according to St. Gregory of Nyssa, the morning is the most seasonable time for prayer because, says the saint, when prayer precedes business, sin will not find entrance into the soul. And the Venerable Fr. Charles Carafa, founder of the Congregation of the Pious Workers, used to say that a fervent act of love, made in the morning during meditation, is sufficient to maintain the soul in fervor during the entire day. Prayer, as St. Jerome has written, is also necessary in the evening. Let not the body go to rest before the soul is refreshed by mental prayer, which is the food of the soul. But at all times and in all places, we can pray; it is enough for us to raise the mind to God and to make good acts, for in this consists mental prayer.

2. With regard to the time to be spent in mental prayer, the rule of the saints was to devote to it all the hours that were not necessary for the occupations of human life. St. Francis Borgia employed in meditation eight hours in the day, because his superiors would not allow him a longer time; and when the eight hours had expired, he earnestly asked permission to remain a little longer at prayer, saying, "Ah! Give me another little quarter of an hour." St. Philip Neri was accustomed to spend the entire night in prayer. St. Anthony the Abbot remained the whole night in prayer; and when the sun appeared, which was the time assigned for terminating his prayer, he complained of it for having risen too soon.

Prayer

Fr. Balthassar Alvarez used to say that a soul that loves God, when not in prayer, is like a stone out of its center, in a violent state, for in this life we should, as much as possible imitate the life of the saints in bliss, who are constantly employed in the contemplation of God.

But let us come to the particular time which a religious who seeks perfection should devote to mental prayer. Fr. Torres prescribed an hour's meditation in the morning, another during the day, and a half hour's meditation in the evening, when they should not be hindered by sickness or by any duty of obedience. If to you this appears too much, I counsel you to give at least two hours to mental prayer. It is certain that a half hour's meditation each day would not be sufficient to attain a high degree of perfection; for beginners, however, this would be sufficient.

Sometimes the Lord wishes you to omit prayer in order to perform some work of fraternal charity; but it is necessary to attend to what St. Laurence Justinian says: "When charity requires it, the spouse of Jesus goes to serve her neighbor; but during that time she continually sighs to return to converse with her Spouse in the solitude of her cell."[227] Fr. Vincent Carafa, General of the Society of Jesus, stole as many little moments of time as he could and employed them in prayer.

Mental prayer is tedious to those who are attached to the world, but not to those who love God only. Ah! Conversation with God is not painful or tedious to those who truly love Him. His conversation has no bitterness, His company produces not tediousness, but joy and gladness. Mental prayer, says St. John Climacus, is nothing else than a familiar conversation and union with God. In prayer, as St. Chrysostom says, the soul converses

[227] *De Casto Conn.* c. 12.

with God, and God with the soul. No, the life of holy persons who love prayer, and fly from earthly amusements, is not a life of bitterness. If you do not believe me, "Taste and see that the Lord is sweet" (Ps. 33:9). Try it, and you shall see how sweet the Lord is to those who leave all things in order to converse with Him only. But the end which we ought to propose to ourselves in going to meditation should be, as has been said several times, not spiritual consolation, but to learn from our Lord what He wishes from us and to divest ourselves of all self-love. "To prepare yourself for prayer," says St. John Climacus, "put off your own will." To prepare ourselves well for meditation, we must renounce self-will and say to God, "Speak, Lord, for Thy servant heareth." Lord, tell me what Thou wishest me to do; I am willing to do it. And it is necessary to say this with a resolute will, for without this disposition, the Lord will not speak to us.

Chapter 6

⋯•⊂•●•⊃•⋯

The Manner of Making Mental Prayer

Mental prayer contains three parts: the Preparation, the Meditation, and the Conclusion.

1. The Preparation

Begin by disposing your mind and body to enter into pious recollection.

Leave at the door of the place where you are going to converse with God all extraneous thoughts, saying, with St. Bernard, O my thoughts, wait here: after prayer we shall speak on other matters. Be careful not to allow the mind to wander where it wishes; but should a distracting thought enter, act as we shall tell you in chapter 7.

The posture of the body most suitable for prayer is to be kneeling, but if this posture becomes so irksome as to cause distractions, we may, as St. John of the Cross says, make our meditation while modestly sitting down.

The Preparation consists of three acts: (1) Act of faith in the presence of God; (2) Act of humility and of contrition; (3) Act of petition for light.

We may perform these acts in the following manner:

Prayer

Act of Faith in the Presence of God, and Act of Adoration

My God, I believe that Thou art here present, and I adore Thee with my whole soul. Amen.

Be careful to make this act with a lively faith, for a lively remembrance of the divine presence contributes greatly to remove distractions. Cardinal Carracciolo, bishop of Aversa, used to say that when a person is distracted in prayer, there is reason to think that he has not made a lively act of faith.

Act of Humility and of Contrition

Lord, I should now be in Hell in punishment of the offenses I have given Thee. I am sorry for them from the bottom of my heart; have mercy on me. Amen.

Act of Petition for Light

Eternal Father, for the sake of Jesus and Mary, give me light in this meditation, that I may draw fruit from it. Amen.

We must then recommend ourselves to the Blessed Virgin by saying a Hail Mary, to St. Joseph, to our Guardian Angel, and to our holy patron.

These acts, says St. Francis de Sales, ought to be made with fervor but should be short that we may pass immediately to the meditation.

2. The Meditation

When you make meditation privately, you may always use some book, at least at the commencement, and stop when you find yourself most touched. St. Francis de Sales says that in this we would do as the bees that stop on a flower as long as they find any honey on it and then pass on to another. St. Teresa used a book for seventeen years; she would first read a little, then meditate for a short time on what she had read. It is useful to meditate in this manner, in imitation of the pigeon that first drinks and then raises its eyes to Heaven.

When mental prayer is made in common, one person reads for the rest the subject of meditation and divides it into two parts: the first is read at the beginning, after the preparatory acts; the second, toward the middle of the half hour, or after the Consecration if the meditation is made during the Mass. One should read in a loud tone of voice and slowly, so as to be well understood.

It should be remembered that the advantage of mental prayer consists not so much in meditating as in making affections, petitions, and resolutions: these are the three principal fruits of meditation. "The progress of a soul," says St. Teresa, "does not consist in thinking much of God, but in loving Him ardently; and this love is acquired by resolving to do a great deal for Him."[228] Speaking of mental prayer, the spiritual masters say that meditation is, as it were, the needle which, when it has passed, must be succeeded by the golden thread, composed, as has been said, of affections, petitions, and resolutions; and this we are going to explain.

The Affections

When you have reflected on the point of meditation and feel any pious sentiment, raise your heart to God and offer Him acts of humility, of confidence, or of thanksgiving; but, above all, repeat in mental prayer acts of contrition and of love.

[228] *Book of the Foundations*, ch. 5.

Prayer

The act of love, as also the act of contrition, is the golden chain that binds the soul to God. An act of perfect charity is sufficient for the remission of all our sins: "Charity covereth a multitude of sins" (1 Pet. 4:8). The Lord has declared that He cannot hate the soul that loves Him: "I love them that love me" (Prov. 8:17). The Venerable Sr. Mary Crucified once saw a globe of fire in which some straws that had been thrown into it were instantly consumed. By this vision she was given to understand that a soul, by making a true act of love, obtains the remission of all its faults. Besides, the Angelic Doctor teaches that by every act of love we acquire a new degree of glory. "Every act of charity merits eternal life" (I-II, q. 114, art. 7).

Acts of love may be made in the following manner:

My God, I esteem Thee more than all things.

I love Thee with my whole heart. I delight in Thy felicity.

I would wish to see Thee loved by all. I wish only what Thou wishest.

Make known to me what Thou wishest from me, and I will do it.

Dispose as Thou pleasest of me and of all that I possess. Amen.

This last act of oblation is particularly dear to God.

In meditation, among the acts of love toward God, there is none more perfect than taking delight in the infinite joy of God. This is certainly the continual exercise of the blessed in Heaven; so that he who often rejoices in the joy of God begins in this life to do that which he hopes to do in Heaven through all eternity.

It may be useful here to remark, with St. Augustine, that it is not the torture, but the cause, which makes the martyr. Whence St. Thomas, in his *Summa Theologica*, teaches that martyrdom is to suffer death in the exercise of an act of virtue. From which we may infer that not only he who by the hands of the executioner lays down his life for the Faith, but whoever dies to comply with the divine will, and to please God, is a martyr, since, in sacrificing himself to the divine love, he performs an act of the most exalted virtue. We all have to pay the great debt of nature; let us therefore endeavor, in holy prayer, to obtain resignation to the divine will — to receive death and every tribulation in conformity with the dispensations of His Providence. As often as we shall perform this act of resignation with sufficient fervor, we may hope to be made partakers of the merits of the martyrs. St. Mary Magdalene, in reciting the doxology, always bowed her head in the same spirit as she would have done in receiving the stroke of the executioner.

Remember that we here speak of the ordinary mental prayer; for should anyone feel himself at any time united with God by supernatural or infused recollection, without any particular thought of an eternal truth or of any divine mystery, he should not then labor to perform any other acts than those to which he feels himself sweetly drawn to God. It is then enough to endeavor, with loving attention, to remain united with God, without impeding the divine operation, or forcing himself to make reflections and acts. But this is to be understood when the Lord calls the soul to this supernatural prayer; but until we receive such a call, we should not depart from the ordinary method of mental prayer but should, as has been said, make use of meditation and affections. However, for persons accustomed to mental prayer, it is better to employ themselves in affections than in consideration.

Prayer

Petitions

Moreover, in mental prayer it is very profitable, and perhaps more useful than any other act, to repeat petitions to God, asking, with humility and confidence, His graces; that is, His light, resignation, perseverance, and the like; but, above all, the gift of His holy love. St. Francis de Sales used to say that by obtaining the dvine love we obtain all graces; for a soul that truly loves God with its whole heart will, of itself, without being admonished by others, abstain from giving Him the smallest displeasure and will labor to please Him to the best of its ability.

When you find yourself in aridity and darkness, so that you feel, as it were, incapable of making good acts, it is sufficient to say:

> My Jesus, mercy.
> Lord, for the sake of Thy mercy, assist me.

And the meditation made in this manner will be for you perhaps the most useful and fruitful.

The Venerable Paul Segneri used to say that until he studied theology, he employed himself during the time of mental prayer in making reflections and affections; but "God" (these are his own words) "afterward opened my eyes, and thenceforward I endeavored to employ myself in petitions; and if there is any good in me, I ascribe it to this exercise of recommending myself to God." Do you likewise do the same; ask of God His graces, in the name of Jesus Christ, and you will obtain whatsoever you desire. This Our Savior has promised, and His promise cannot fail: "Amen, amen, I say to you, if you ask the Father anything in my name, He will give it you" (John 16:23).

In a word, all mental prayer should consist in acts and petitions. Hence, the Venerable Sr. Mary Crucified, while in an ecstasy, declared that mental prayer is the respiration of the soul; for, as by respiration, the air is first attracted, and afterward given back, so, by petitions, the soul first receives grace from God, and then, by good acts of oblation and love, it gives itself to Him.

Resolutions

In terminating the meditation it is necessary to make a particular resolution; as, for example, to avoid some particular defect into which you have more frequently fallen, or to practice some virtue, such as to suffer the annoyance which you receive from another person, to obey more exactly a certain superior, or to perform some particular act of mortification. We must repeat the same resolution several times, until we find that we have got rid of the defect or acquired the virtue. Afterward, reduce to practice the resolutions you have made, as soon as an occasion is presented. You would also do well, before the conclusion of your prayer, to renew the vows or any particular engagement by vow or otherwise that you have made with God. This renewal is most pleasing to God if we multiply the merit of the good work and draw down upon us a new help in order to persevere and to grow in grace.

The Conclusion

The conclusion of meditation consists of three acts:
1. In thanking God for the lights received
2. In making a purpose to fulfill the resolutions made
3. In asking of the Eternal Father, for the sake of Jesus and Mary, grace to be faithful to them

Be careful never to omit, at the end of meditation, to recommend to God the souls in Purgatory and poor sinners. St. John Chrysostom says that nothing more clearly shows our love for Jesus Christ than our zeal in recommending our brethren to Him.

Prayer

St. Francis de Sales remarks that in leaving mental prayer, we should take with us a nosegay of flowers, in order to smell them during the day; that is, we should remember one or two points in which we have felt particular devotion, in order to excite our fervor during the day.

The ejaculations which are dearest to God are those of love, of resignation, of oblation of ourselves. Let us endeavor not to perform any action without first offering it to God and not to allow at the most a quarter of an hour to pass, in whatever occupations we may find ourselves, without raising the heart to the Lord by some good act. Moreover, in our leisure time, such as when we are waiting for a person, or when we walk in the garden, or are confined to bed by sickness, let us endeavor, to the best of our ability, to unite ourselves to God. It is also necessary by observing silence, by seeking solitude as much as possible, and by remembering the presence of God, to preserve the pious sentiments conceived in meditation.

Chapter 7

Distractions and Aridities

Distractions

If, after having well prepared ourselves for mental prayer, as has been explained in the preceding pages, a distracting thought should enter, we must not be disturbed nor seek to banish it with a violent effort; but let us remove it calmly and return to God. Let us remember that the devil labors hard to disturb us in the time of meditation, in order to make us abandon it. Let him, then, who omits mental prayer on account of distractions be persuaded that he gives delight to the devil. It is impossible, says Cassian, that our minds should be free from all distractions during prayer.

Let us, then, never give up meditation, however great our distractions may be. St. Francis de Sales says that if, in mental prayer, we should do nothing else than continually banish distractions and temptations, the meditation would be well made. Before him, St. Thomas, in his *Summa Theologica*, taught that involuntary distractions do not take away the fruit of mental prayer. Finally, when we perceive that we are deliberately distracted, let us desist from the voluntary defect and banish the distraction, but let us be careful not to discontinue our meditation.

Prayer

Aridities

The greatest pain of souls in meditation is to find themselves sometimes without a feeling of devotion, weary of it, and without any sensible desire of loving God; and with this is joined the fear of being in the wrath of God through their sins, on account of which the Lord has abandoned them; and being in this gloomy darkness, they know not how to escape from it, it seeming to them that every way is closed against them.

When a soul gives itself up to the spiritual life, the Lord is accustomed to heap consolations upon it, in order to wean it from the pleasures of the world, but afterward, when He sees it more settled in spiritual ways, He draws back His hand, in order to make proof of its love and to see whether it serves and loves God unrecompensed, while in this world, with spiritual joys. Some foolish persons, seeing themselves in a state of aridity, think that God may have abandoned them; or, again, that the spiritual life was not made for them; and so they leave off prayer and lose all that they have gained.

In order to be a soul of prayer, man must resist with fortitude all temptations to discontinue mental prayer in the time of aridity. St. Teresa has left us very excellent instructions on this point. In one place she says, "The devil knows that he has lost the soul that perseveringly practices mental prayer." In another place she says, "I hold for certain that the Lord will conduct to the haven of salvation the soul that perseveres in mental prayer, in spite of all the sins that the devil may oppose."

Again, she says, "He who does not stop in the way of mental prayer reaches the end of his journey, though he should delay a little." Finally, she concludes, saying, "By aridity and temptations the Lord proves His lovers; though aridity should last for life, let not the soul give up prayer; the time will come when all shall be well rewarded."

The Angelic Doctor says that the devotion consists not in feeling, but in the desire and resolution to embrace promptly all that God wills. Such was the prayer that Jesus Christ made in the Garden of Olives; it was full of aridity and tediousness, but it was the most devout and meritorious prayer that had ever been offered in this world. It consisted in these words: My Father, not what I will, but what Thou wilt.

Hence, never give up mental prayer in the time of aridity. Should the tediousness which assails you be very great, divide your meditation into several parts, and employ yourself, for the most part, in petitions to God, even though you should seem to pray without confidence and without fruit. It will be sufficient to say and to repeat: "My Jesus, mercy. Lord, have mercy on us." Pray, and doubt not that God will hear you and grant your petition.

In going to meditation, never propose to yourself your own pleasure and satisfaction, but only to please God and to learn what He wishes you to do. And, for this purpose, pray always that God may make known to you His will and that He may give you strength to fulfill it. All that we ought to seek in mental prayer is light to know, and strength to accomplish, the will of God in our regard.

Prayer

Ah, my Jesus, it appears that Thou couldst do nothing more in order to gain the love of men. It is enough to know that Thou hast wished to become man; that is, to become, like us, a worm. Thou hast wished to lead a painful life, of thirty-three years, amid sorrow and ignominies, and in the end to die on an infamous gibbet. Thou hast also wished to remain under the appearance of bread, in order to become the food of our souls;

Prayer

and how is it possible that Thou hast received so much ingratitude, even from Christians who believe these truths and still love Thee so little. Unhappy me! I have hitherto been among those ungrateful souls; I have attended only to my pleasures and have been forgetful of Thee and of Thy love. I now know the evil I have done; but I repent of it with my whole heart: my Jesus, pardon me. I now love Thee; I love Thee so ardently that I choose death, and a thousand deaths, rather than cease to love Thee. I thank Thee for the light which Thou givest me. Give me strength, O God of my soul, always to advance in Thy love. Accept this poor heart to love Thee. It is true that it has once despised Thee, but now it is enamored of Thy goodness; it loves Thee and desires only to love Thee. O Mary, Mother of God, assist me; in thy intercession I place great confidence. Amen.

Chapter 8

Prayers of St. Alphonsus

Prayer to Obtain Final Perseverance

Eternal Father, I humbly adore and thank Thee for having created me and for having redeemed me by means of Jesus Christ. I thank Thee for having made me a Christian by giving me the true Faith and by adopting me for Thy child in holy Baptism. I thank Thee for having given me time for repentance after my many sins and for having, as I hope, pardoned all my offenses against Thee. O Infinite Goodness! I thank Thee also for having preserved me from falling again as often as I should have done if Thou hadst not held me up and saved me. But my enemies do not cease to fight against me, nor will they until death, that they may again have me for their slave; if Thou dost not keep and help me continually by Thine assistance, I shall be wretched enough to lose Thy grace anew. I therefore pray Thee, for the love of Jesus Christ, to grant me holy perseverance till death. Thy Son Jesus has promised that Thou wilt grant us whatever we ask for in His name. By the merits, then, of Jesus Christ, I beg of Thee for myself, and for all those who are in Thy grace, the grace of never more being separated from Thy love, but that we may always love Thee in this life and in the next.

Mary, Mother of God, pray to Jesus for me. Amen.

Prayer to Jesus Christ to Obtain His Holy Love

My crucified Love, my dear Jesus! I believe in Thee and confess Thee to be the true Son of God and my Savior. I adore Thee from the abyss of my own nothingness, and I thank Thee for the death Thou didst suffer for me, that I might obtain the life of divine grace. My beloved Redeemer, to Thee I owe all my salvation. Through Thee I have hitherto escaped Hell; through Thee have I received the pardon of my sins. But I am so ungrateful that, instead of loving Thee, I have repeated my offenses against Thee. I deserve to be condemned, so as not to be able to love Thee any more. But no, my Jesus, punish me in any other way, but not in this. If I have not loved Thee in time past, I love Thee now; and I desire nothing but to love Thee with all my heart. But without Thy help I can do nothing. Since Thou dost command me to love Thee, give me also the strength to fulfill this Thy sweet and loving precept. Thou has promised to grant all that we ask of Thee: "You shall ask whatever you will, and it shall be done unto you."

Confiding, then, in this promise, my dear Jesus, I ask, first of all, pardon of all my sins; and I repent, above all things, because I have offended Thee, O

Infinite Goodness! I ask for holy perseverance in Thy grace till my death. But, above all, I ask for the gift of Thy holy love. Ah, my Jesus, my Hope, my Love, my All, inflame me with that love which Thou didst come on earth to enkindle!

For this end, make me always live in conformity with Thy holy will. Enlighten me, that I may understand more and more how worthy Thou art of our love and that I may know the immense love Thou has borne me, especially in giving Thy life for me. Grant, then, that I may love Thee with all my heart and may love Thee always, and never cease to beg of Thee the grace to love Thee in this life; that living always and dying in Thy love, I may come one day to love Thee with all my strength in Heaven, never to leave off loving Thee for all eternity.

O Mother of beautiful love, my advocate and refuge, Mary, who art of all creatures the most beautiful, the most loving, and the most beloved of God, and whose only desire it is to see Him loved! Ah, by the love thou bearest to Jesus Christ, pray for me and obtain for me the grace to love Him always and with all my heart! This I ask and hope for from thee. Amen.

Prayer to Obtain Confidence in the Merits of Jesus Christ and in the Intercession of Mary

Eternal Father, I thank Thee for myself, and on behalf of all mankind, for the great mercy that Thou hast shown us, in sending Thy Son to be made man and to

Prayer

die to obtain our salvation; I thank Thee for it, and
I should wish to offer Thee in thanksgiving all that
love which is due for such an inestimable benefit. By
His merits our sins are pardoned, and Thy justice is
satisfied for the punishment we had merited; by these
merits Thou dost receive us miserable sinners into Thy
grace, while we deserve nothing but hatred and chas-
tisement, Thou dost receive men to reign in Paradise.
Finally, Thou hast bound Thyself, in consideration of
these merits, to grant all gifts and graces to those who
ask for them in the name of Jesus Christ.

I thank Thee also, O Infinite Goodness, that, in order to strengthen our confidence, besides giving us Jesus
Christ as our Redeemer, Thou hast also given us Thy
beloved daughter Mary as our advocate; so that, with
that heart full of mercy which Thou hast given her, she
may never cease to succor by her intercession any sinner who may have recourse to her; and this intercession
is so powerful with Thee that Thou canst not deny her
any grace which she asks of Thee.

Hence it is Thy will that we should have a great
confidence in the merits of Jesus and in the intercession of Mary. But this confidence is Thy gift, and it is a
great gift which Thou dost grant to those only who ask
Thee for it. This confidence, then, in the Blood of Jesus
Christ, and in the patronage of Mary, I beg of Thee,
through the merits of Jesus and Mary.

To Thee, also, my dear Redeemer, do I turn; it was
to obtain for me this confidence in Thy merits that
Thou didst sacrifice Thy life on the Cross for me, who
was worthy only of punishment. Accomplish, then, the

end for which Thou hast died; enable me to hope for all things, through confidence in Thy Passion.

And thou, O Mary, my Mother and my hope after Jesus, obtain for me a firm confidence, first in the merits of Jesus thy Son, and then in the intercession of thy prayers — prayers which are all-powerful in gaining all they ask!

O my beloved Jesus! O sweet Mary! I trust in Thee. To Thee do I give my soul; Thou doth love it so much, have pity on it, and save it. Amen.

<hr />

Prayer to Obtain the Grace of Being Constant in Prayer

O God of my soul, I hope in Thy goodness that Thou hast pardoned all my offenses against Thee and that I am now in a state of grace. I thank Thee for it with all my heart, and I hope to thank Thee for all eternity. I know that I have fallen, because I have not had recourse to Thee when I was tempted, to ask for holy perseverance. For the future, I firmly resolve to recommend myself always to Thee, and especially when I see myself in danger of again offending Thee. I will always fly to Thy mercy, invoking always the most holy names of Jesus and Mary, with full confidence that when I pray Thou, wilt not fail to give me the strength which I have not of myself to resist my enemies. This I resolve and promise to do. But of what use, O my God, will all these resolutions and promises be if Thou dost not assist me with Thy grace to put them in practice; that is, to have recourse to Thee in all dangers? Ah, Eternal Father! Help me, for the love of

Prayer

Jesus Christ; and let me never omit recommending my-self to Thee whenever I am tempted. I know that Thou dost always help me when I have recourse to Thee; but my fear is that I should forget to recommend myself to Thee, and so my negligence will be the cause of my ruin, that is, the loss of Thy grace, the greatest evil that can happen to me. Ah, by the merits of Jesus Christ, give me grace to pray to Thee; but grant me such an abundant grace that I may always pray, and pray as I ought!

O my Mother Mary, whenever I have had recourse to thee, thou hast obtained for me the help which has kept me from falling! Now I come to beg of thee to ob-tain a still greater grace, namely, that of recommending myself always to thy Son and to thee in all my necessi-ties. My Queen, thou obtainest all thou dost desire from God by the love thou bearest to Jesus Christ; obtain for me now this grace which I beg of thee, namely, to pray always and never to cease praying till I die. Amen.

◄◄──◅◦●◦▻──►►

Prayer to Be Said Every Day,
to Obtain the Graces Necessary for Salvation

Eternal Father, Thy Son hast promised that Thou wilt grant us all the graces which we ask Thee for in His name. In the name, therefore, and by the merits of Jesus Christ, I ask the following graces for myself and for all mankind. And, first, I pray Thee to give me a lively faith in all that the holy Roman Church teaches me. Enlighten me also, that I may know the vanity of the goods of this world, and the immensity of the infinite good that Thou art; make me also see the deformity of the sins I have committed, that I may humble myself and detest them as I ought, and, on the other hand, show me how worthy Thou art by reason of Thy goodness, that I should love Thee with all my heart. Make me know also the love Thou hast borne me, that from this day forward I may try to be grateful for so much goodness. Secondly, give me a firm confidence in Thy mercy of receiving the pardon of my sins, holy perseverance, and, finally, the glory of Paradise, through the merits of Jesus Christ and the intercession of Mary. Thirdly, give me a great love toward Thee, which shall detach me from the love of this world and of myself, so that I may love none other but Thee and that I may neither do nor desire anything else but what is for Thy glory. Fourthly, I beg of Thee a perfect resignation to Thy will, in accepting with tranquility sorrows, infirmities, contempt, persecutions, aridity of spirit, loss of property, of esteem, of relatives, and every other cross which shall come to me from Thy hands. I offer myself entirely to Thee, that Thou mayest do with me and all that belongs to me what Thou pleasest. Do Thou only give me light and strength to do Thy will; and especially at the hour of death help me to sacrifice my life to Thee with all the affection I am capable of, in union with the sacrifice which Thy Son Jesus Christ made of His life on the Cross on Calvary. Fifthly, I beg of Thee a great sorrow for my sins, which may make me grieve over them as long as I live, and weep for the insults I have offered Thee, the Sovereign Good, who art worthy of infinite love, and who hast loved me so much.

Prayer

Sixthly, I pray Thee to give me the spirit of true humility and meekness, that I may accept with peace, and even with joy, all the contempt, ingratitude, and ill-treatment that I may receive. At the same time, I also pray Thee to give me perfect charity, which shall make me wish well to those who have done evil to me and to do what good I can, at least by praying, for those who have in any way injured me. Seventhly, I beg of Thee to give me a love for the virtue of holy mortification, by which I may chastise my rebellious senses and cross my self-love; at the same time, I beg Thee to give me holy purity of body and the grace to resist all bad temptations, by ever having recourse to Thee and Thy most holy Mother. Give me grace faithfully to obey my spiritual father and all my superiors in all things. Give me an upright intention, that in all I desire and do I may seek only Thy glory and to please Thee alone. Give me a great confidence in the Passion of Jesus Christ and in the intercession of Mary Immaculate. Give me a great love toward the most Adorable Sacrament of the Altar and a tender devotion to and love for Thy holy Mother. Give me, I pray Thee, above all, holy perseverance and the grace always to pray for it, especially in time of temptation and at the hour of death.

Lastly, I recommend to Thee the holy souls of Purgatory, my relatives and benefactors; and in an especial manner I recommend to Thee all those who hate me or who have in any way offended me; I beg of Thee to render them good for the evil they have done or may wish to do me. Finally, I recommend to Thee all infidels, heretics, and all poor sinners; give them light and strength to deliver themselves from sin. O most loving God, make Thyself known and loved by all, but especially by those who have been more ungrateful to Thee than others, so that by Thy goodness I may come one day to sing Thy mercies in Paradise; for my hope is in the merits of Thy Blood and in the patronage of Mary.

O Mary, Mother of God, pray to Jesus for me! So I hope; so may it be! Amen.

◦◦• ◁•◦•▷ •◦◦

Aspirations and Thoughts

O God! Who knows what fate awaits me?

I shall be either eternally happy or eternally miserable.

Of what worth is all the world without God? Let all be lost, but let not God be lost. I love Thee, my Jesus, who didst die for me! Would that I had died before I ever offended Thee!

I will rather die than lose God.

Jesus and Mary, Thou art my hope.

My God, help me, for the love of Jesus Christ!

My Jesus, Thou alone art sufficient for me!

Suffer me not to separate myself from Thee.

Give me Thy love, and then do with me what Thou pleasest.

Prayer

Whom shall I love, if I love not Thee, my God?

Eternal Father, help me, for the love of Jesus!

I believe in Thee, I hope in Thee, I love Thee!

Here I am, O Lord; do with me what Thou wilt!

When shall I see myself altogether Thine, my God?

When shall I be able to say to Thee, My
God, I can lose Thee no more?

Mary, my hope, have pity on me!

Mother of God, pray to Jesus for me!

Lord, who am I, that Thou shouldst
desire to be loved by me?

My God, I desire Thee alone, and nothing more.

I desire all that Thou dost will, and that alone.

Oh, that I might be annihilated for Thee,
who wast annihilated for me!

Toward Thee alone, my God, have I been ungrateful!

I have offended Thee enough, I will no longer displease Thee.

If I had died then, I could not have loved Thee any more.

Let me die before again offending Thee.

Thou hast waited for me that I might
love Thee. Yea, I will love Thee.

I consecrate the remainder of my life to Thee.

O my Jesus, draw me entirely to Thyself!

Thou wilt not leave me; I will not leave Thee.

I hope that we shall always love each other, O God of my soul!

My Jesus, make me all Thine before I die!

Grant that when Thou shalt come to judge me, I
may see Thee with a benign countenance.

Thou hast done more than enough to oblige me
to love Thee. I love Thee, I love Thee!

Deign to accept the love of a sinner
who has so often offended Thee.

Thou has given Thyself all to me; I give myself all to Thee.

I desire to love Thee exceedingly in this life
that I may love Thee exceedingly in the next.

Prayer

Teach me to know Thy great goodness,
that I may love Thee very much.

Thou lovest those who love Thee. I love
Thee, do Thou also love me.

Give me the love Thou requirest of me.
I rejoice that Thou art infinitely happy.

Oh, that I had always loved Thee and had
died before I had offended Thee.

Grant that I may overcome all things to please Thee.

I give Thee my whole will; dispose of me as Thou pleasest.

My pleasure is to please Thee, O Infinite Goodness!

I hope to love Thee for all eternity, O eternal God!

Thou art omnipotent; make me a saint.

Thou didst seek me while I was flying from Thee; Thou
wilt not drive me away now that I seek after Thee.

I thank Thee for giving me time to love
Thee. I thank Thee, and love Thee!

Let me give myself entirely to Thee this day;
punish me in any way, but deprive me
not of the power of loving Thee.

I will love Thee, my God, without reserve.

I accept all sufferings and all contempt,
provided I may love Thee.

I desire to die for Thee, who didst die for me.

I wish that all could love Thee, who didst die for me.

I wish that all could love Thee as Thou meritest.

I wish to do everything that I know to be Thy pleasure.

I care more to please Thee than for all
the pleasures of the world.

O holy will of God, Thou art my love!

O Mary, draw me entirely to God!

O my Mother, make me always have
recourse to thee; it is for thee to make me
a saint; this is my hope. Amen.

About the Author

St. Alphonsus was born into the noble house of Liguori in 1696. Well educated and talented from an early age, he studied law at the University of Naples and received his doctorate when he was only sixteen. He earned success as a lawyer, eventually becoming one of the leaders of the Neapolitan Bar. A turning point came in Alphonsus's life, however, when he overlooked a point in a case that rendered his entire argument unsound. Crushed and humiliated by this mistake, he abandoned the practice of law, never to return. This incident showed the young lawyer the vanity and folly of worldly affairs, and he resolved to dedicate his life entirely to God.

Despite his father's bitter opposition, Alphonsus entered the priesthood and was ordained in 1726. In 1732, he founded the Congregation of the Most Holy Redeemer, also known as the Redemptorists. He was made a bishop in 1762.

Alphonsus vowed never to waste a moment of his time, and he fulfilled this promise to a heroic degree. "I never remember," said one of his companions, "to have seen Alphonsus waste a moment when he lived with us. He was always preaching, or hearing confessions, or at prayer or study." Alphonsus wrote more than a hundred books. He died in 1787 and was declared a Doctor of the Church by Pope Pius IX in 1871.

Alphonsus was filled with a great zeal for souls. His eloquent sermons, wise teachings, and kindness as a confessor won many souls for Christ. "In God you possess the most exalted and supreme Lord," he wrote in his book *How to Pray at All Times* (1753), "but also a Friend who loves you with the greatest possible love. He is not offended—on the contrary He is pleased—when you treat Him with that confidence, freedom, and tenderness with which a child treats its mother." Through his inspiring words and instructive teaching, St. Alphonsus's enduring works continue to show souls how to develop such friendship with God.

Sophia Institute

Sophia Institute is a nonprofit institution that seeks to nurture the spiritual, moral, and cultural life of souls and to spread the Gospel of Christ in conformity with the authentic teachings of the Roman Catholic Church.

Sophia Institute Press fulfills this mission by offering translations, reprints, and new publications that afford readers a rich source of the enduring wisdom of mankind.

Sophia Institute also operates the popular online resource CatholicExchange.com. *Catholic Exchange* provides world news from a Catholic perspective as well as daily devotionals and articles that will help readers to grow in holiness and live a life consistent with the teachings of the Church.

In 2013, Sophia Institute launched Sophia Institute for Teachers to renew and rebuild Catholic culture through service to Catholic education. With the goal of nurturing the spiritual, moral, and cultural life of souls, and an abiding respect for the role and work of teachers, we strive to provide materials and programs that are at once enlightening to the mind and ennobling to the heart; faithful and complete, as well as useful and practical.

Sophia Institute gratefully recognizes the Solidarity Association for preserving and encouraging the growth of our apostolate over the course of many years. Without their generous and timely support, this book would not be in your hands.

www.SophiaInstitute.com
www.CatholicExchange.com
www.SophiaInstituteforTeachers.org